Balinese Music

Balinese Music

– by –

MICHAEL TENZER

PERIPLUS
EDITIONS

ILLUSTRATIONS:
I Made Moja

PHOTOGRAPHS:
Rio Helmi: pages 18, 26-27, 72-73, 74,
82, 83, 87, 88, 90, 92, 95, 108, 120
Tom Ballinger: pages 2, 10, 12, 28, 44, 45,
48, 56, 85, 96, 102, 106, 122, 125
K. Prasetya: pages 112, 116, 117
Kal Muller: pages 40, 51
Eric Oey: pages 30, 94
Hans Höfer: pages 8-9
Mike Hosken: page 79

DISTRIBUTORS:
Indonesia: PT Wira Mandala Pustaka (Java Books - Indonesia)
Jl. Kelapa Gading Kirana, Blok A-14 No. 17, Jakarta 14240

Singapore and Malaysia: Berkeley Books Pte. Ltd.
5 Little Road #08-01, Singapore 536983

United States of America: Charles E. Tuttle Co., Inc.
RRI Box 231-5, North Clarendon, VT 05759-9700

Page 2: *Gongs are at the heart of the Balinese gamelan tradition.*
Pages 8-9: *Gamelan Gong Kebyar, Pengosekan village.*

PRINTED IN SINGAPORE

Contents

Preface

IN 1976, as a young composer in college, not quite out of my teens and with a healthy appetite for aural stimulus, I chanced to overhear an animated conversation between a wonderful jazz pianist whom I knew and another friend. I was just walking by, but caught the phrase "gamelan music," preceded by a string of superlatives. The word "gamelan" sparked something in me, even though I had never heard it before. Turning on my heels I headed to the local record store and bought the only gamelan release that I could find—a record of Balinese music on the Nonesuch label—and made for my dorm room. Before taking off my coat I put the disc on the stereo and turned up the volume. I felt my eyes opening very wide and was quickly swept into a state of intense concentration. Within ten minutes I had made a pact with myself to go to Bali and learn how to make the beautiful and challenging sounds that were rushing out of the speakers. (Much later, I learned that my friend had actually been speaking about the Javanese gamelan, which never would have captivated me as the Balinese did. I've always considered my mistake in the record store to be a great stroke of luck.)

A year hence, on my twentieth birthday, I stepped off the ferry from Banyuwangi, in East Java, to find myself staring up at an enormous temple gate in Gilimanuk, in West Bali. It was almost midnight and I had been traveling for three days, including a long stretch of a slow, hot train. I was already delirious from a list of illnesses and but dimly aware that I had to lug my bags onto a bus now rumbling towards me—for a three hour ride to Denpasar. But the night was clear, and I still remember how the gate seemed to welcome me.

I had brought a few letters of introduction and had some contacts. Settling in Peliatan village at the home of the painter Ketut Madra, I began music lessons with Nyoman Sumandhi at the KOKAR High School of Music and Dance. My first studies were the Baris melody, ornamentation, and drumming which is presented here in Chapter 5. Sumandhi entreated me to feel like family, taking me under his wing and all over Bali on the back of his Honda. It was not long before I was having lengthy lessons twice daily. In the six months I was there, my language skills sputtered and finally began to rev. Evenings I composed, borrowing from what my teachers had taught me. My delight in the music quickly earned me many musician friends. Without quite knowing what I would do with them, I bought a set of instruments to bring back to the States.

Arriving in Berkeley, California in the fall of 1979 with my instruments in tow, I began graduate school in Western music. I joined up with my friends Rachel Cooper and the Balinese drummer I Wayan Suweca to found a gamelan organization. We modeled ourselves on the community-based musical clubs of Bali, and attracted many enthusiastic members. I still marvel at the music's ability to take root so removed from its natural environs. Suweca stayed for two years, but after he went home the group—which he had named Sekar Jaya (Victorious Flower)—continued to support residencies for a string of Balinese musicians and dancers. One thing had led to another. I had succeeded in surrounding myself with Balinese music as if it were a cocoon, both at home and in Bali. I have been back to Indonesia for more many times since.

My years of experience with this music have turned me into an enthusiastic disseminator, in reverence of this artistic tradition and the people and culture that possess it. No music in the world can corner the market on beauty, sophistication, subtlety or any other aesthetic identity, but Balinese music does possess a singular mix of orchestral complexity and a strong commitment to group interaction that makes it inspirational. Balinese gamelans rehearse to perfect their music more than any other large ensembles in the world. The process with which the music is made creates a unique personal bond between members of the group, which is precisely what playing music should be all about.

There are so many Balinese teachers and friends who I want to thank and write about here, all of whom have enriched me and inspired me, but there is only room to list their names. They include Ni Ketut Arini Alit, Ketut Gde Asnawa, I Wayan Gama Astawa, I Komang Astita, I Made Bandem, Ni Luh Swasthi Bandem, Dewa Nyoman Batuan, I Wayan Beratha, I Made Canderi, I Nyoman Catra, I Made Demong, I Wayan Dibia, I Made Gableran, I Wayan Gandera, I Ketut Gantas, I Made Grindem, Anak Agung Putu Griya, I Made Griya, Cokorda Alit Hendrawan, I Wayan Jebeg, I Made Jimat, Ni Wayan Konderi, I Wayan Konolan, I Ketut Kumpul, Desak Made Laksmi, Ni Putu Lastini, I Made Lebah, I Wayan Loceng, I Gusti Lumbung, I Ketut Madra, Anak Agung Gde Mandera, Gde Manik, Cokorda Mas, Ida Bagus Raka Negara, I Gusti Ngurah Panji, I Wayan Pogog, I Wayan Rai, Ida Bagus Aji Made Regog, I Nyoman Rembang, I Ketut Rintig, Ni Wayan Roni, Anak Agung Raka Saba, I Wayan Sinti, Ni Gusti Ayu Srinatih, I Wayan Sujana, I Nyoman Sumandhi, Ni Ketut Suryatini, I Made Suta, I Wayan Suweca, I Ketut Tama, I Wayan Tembres, I Ketut Tutur, Nanik Wenten, I Nyoman Wenten, I Nyoman Windha, I Wayan Wira, Ni Made Wiratini, and many, many others. There has not been room to credit individual informants for their contributions during the course of the text.

In addition, what I learned from these artists might never have grown inside of me had it not been for the musicians of Gamelan Sekar Jaya, with whom I shared year after year of high adventure. The same holds for members of Gamelan Sekar Kembar in New Haven, Connecticut, who demonstrated a quickness and enthusiasm that surprised even some jaded Balinese experts. Other teachers and friends of the music to whom expressions of gratitude are due include Frank Bennett, Martin Bresnick, Mantle Hood, Dieter Mack, David Mott, Danker Schaareman, Andrew Toth, Andreas Varsanyi and Bonnie Wade.

Finally, thanks also to my parents, my fantastic wife Pam, and, at last, Molly.

Michael Tenzer
Hamden, Connecticut

Oleg Tambulilingan, a dance created in the 1950s, performed with gamelan gong kebyar.

CHAPTER ONE

An Introduction to Balinese Music

"IT is the opening day of the temple feast, and the children have assembled at the house to carry their gamelan to the temple. I give them each a cloth of large black and white check for a headdress, which will mark them as a club, and they all proceed to pick bright red blossoms from the hibiscus shrubs and put them in their hair. They then take their instruments and go out in dignified single file, while I follow behind. On the way to the temple someone suddenly remembers that the gamelan has never been blessed and purified. This is a bad start, but, on reaching the temple, we find that it can be done on the spot, for there are both priest and holy water, and we may have the benefit of offerings already prepared for other purposes. The arrival of the gamelan has caused much excited comment. The other club is already there, and the two gamelan are set in opposite pavilions. The ceremony of blessing the instruments is performed, and the children are told to play one piece as a termination of the rite. They sit down, and people eagerly crowd around, their curiosity aroused by the size of the children and the presence of the surprising *angklung*. The priest asks them to stand back. It is the children's hour; they dominate the scene. The women pause in their offerings and stand by; the adult club watches from the pavilion. The priest says '*Enggeh, tabuhin!* (Well, strike up!)' and the children begin, while everyone listens in silence, smiling with pleasure. Suddenly for once, the Balinese seem almost sentimental. There is no doubt that the children are a success."

— The American musician Colin McPhee, describing the debut of a children's music club that he sponsored in Sayan village, Bali, 1938.[1]

Music lovers have long discerned a splendid aural feast in the sounds of the *gamelan*. Emanating perpetually from communities all over the island of Bali, its sonorities sail over the ricefields on clear nights, showering the air with brilliant cascades of metallic sound, lonely whispering melodies, grandiose and clangorous marches, virtuosic rhythms, and breathtaking crescendos. Animated with the sounds of drums, flutes and gongs, it is a compelling experience that persists in

[1] from McPhee, Colin, "Children and Music in Bali," taken from Belo, Jane, ed. "Traditional Balinese Culture," Columbia University Press, New York 1970. The article was originally written in 1939 for the periodical *Djawa*; it was subsequently revised in 1954.

Gamelan angklung performing at a temple ceremony in the village of Kedewatan.

the mind's ear long after its pulsations fade.

The ethereal music of the gamelan is sustained with an esthetic that prizes beautiful melody and a refined sense of formal design. This is not a music characterized by the sweeping emotions of romanticism; rather it is detailed, secure in construction, and full of insistent rhythms and elegant patterns. In the music's rich abstractions the listener encounters clarity and complexity that make it one of the most rewarding musical experiences to be had on our planet. These rewards are multiplied when one considers the music within the context of the remarkable place and culture that support it, the island of Bali.

Music is ubiquitous in Bali; its abundance is far out of proportion to the dimensions of the island. The Hindu-Balinese religion requires gamelan for the successful completion of most of the tens of thousands of ceremonies undertaken yearly. At a plethora of traditionally mandated religious events, the gods descend in numbers to inhabit their designated shrines for the length of the festivities, awaiting the lavish musical entertainments that their village hosts are expected to provide. For the procession of offerings into the temple, there is music; for the spilling of cremated souls' ashes into the sea, there is music; for the exorcism of evil spirits, there is music; and for the ritual filing of teeth, there is music.

And for dance there is music. In Bali these two art forms are wedded in spirit, nuance, structure and even terminology. Balinese choreography, in its purest interpretation, is a detailed and subtle, physical embodiment of the music that accompanies it. Music and dance together are a mutually reflective duet—

two realizations of the same abstract beauty, each clothed in the attributes of its form. For the gods, dance is as important a part of their visits to the earthly plane as is music. For the Balinese people these two arts are an inexorable combination, and to participate in the performance of either is a coveted privilege.

The Balinese embellish this rigorous schedule of sacred musical events with a wide range of more worldly occasions in which gamelan also assumes a crucial role. There are flirtatious street dances, frenzied bull races, and gamelan performances for guests and dignitaries. A regular cycle of gamelan competitions and festivals provides a forum for people to demonstrate their pride in their musical abilities and their dedication to the cultivation of a priceless cultural heritage for its own sake, independent of the ritual needs that it fills.

Gamelan Music: Sound, Language and Aesthetic

In a general way, the word "gamelan" (pronounced *gah*-meh-lan) means orchestra, or the music played by the orchestra, but it corresponds to the Western sense of that word only in that it conjures up an image of a group of people making music together. To be precise, gamelan refers to the instruments themselves, which exist as an inseparable set, and not to a group of individuals who gather to play upon them. The components of the gamelan come in many combinations, tunings, and sizes, each with specific religious or secular functions. There are almost as many different kinds of gamelans in Bali as there are occasions for them to be heard. The term gamelan itself derives from a Javanese verb meaning 'to handle'; the indigenous Balinese pronunciation has a 'b' at the beginning of the second syllable: *gambelan*. A general term for the art of playing music is *kerawitan*. Gamelan compositions are referred to as *tabuh* (also an older word for the mallets used to play the instruments), *gending*, or *lagu*, which is really an Indonesian word for melody.

At the center of Balinese musical culture are the deep and penetrating reverberations of the bronze gongs. When the raised center, or boss, of a large gong is struck, a powerful bass tone emerges, the sound of which has inspired the reverence of Balinese for centuries. Gongs, as the strongest and most important timbre in most gamelans, legislate the character of the set of instruments to which they belong. A gamelan, so it is said, is only as good as its gong. Enjoying the support of the gong's anchoring are the drums, flutes and keyed metal instruments (metallophones) that comprise the remainder of the ensemble. Most of these instruments are constructed primarily of bronze, but some are made wholly from bamboo, and a few others from more esoteric materials. Each has its own name and definite musical function. Normally they all must play together in order for the music to sound as it should.

Sets of gamelan instruments are usually owned and maintained by village wards called *banjars*, which call upon their citizenry to fill the places in the ensemble. When the members of a gamelan group get together to make music, they do not improvise, except in a few limited cases. They play music that has been fully composed and planned out in advance of rehearsals, learned by rote, and painstakingly practiced, coordinated and polished until the desired musical standard has been achieved. There is little if any room for the individual to express him or herself in gamelan performance; instead the ideal is the cultivation of absolute coordination and channeling of each member's artistic personality into a unified musical expression. The very elements of the music are constructed so as to aid in this process, as we shall see throughout this book.

Just as the building-blocks of the music are illustrative of their larger context, so too are the terms and vocalizations with which the Balinese talk about gamelan and sing its tunes and rhythms. Amongst the hundreds of onomatopoetic words that pepper the indigenous Balinese language (thoroughly distinct from Bahasa Indonesia, the national language) and give it an inherent musicality of its own, there are many that refer to gamelan. The sounds of these words reveals much of importance about Balinese aesthetic concerns and the connections that are perceived between music and natural surroundings. For instance, *tekep* (which sounds almost like t-*k'p* because the consonants are so heavily accented in speech) is a clean and sharp-edged word that denotes the crucial technique of using the fingers to stop the resonance of the bronze keys and gongs in melodic passages. Any gamelan that has not mastered *matetekep* (mah-t'-t'-k'p), the art of tekep-ing, can expect to produce no more than a pathetically unfocussed blur of reverberating bronze.

The words *incep* (in-*che'*) and *resik* (re-*si'*), used to describe the highest degrees of precision and togetherness that a full gamelan ensemble may strive to achieve, are pronounced with marked glottal stops and heavy stresses that mimic the crisp, economical unity that is so highly prized in performance. In contrast, *romon* (roh-*mohn*) and *rontog* (rohn-*tohg*), denoting music so sloppily played that it merits hisses and ridicule, are enunciated with lengthy second syllables that are difficult to utter cleanly. With apologies for dwelling on the negative for a moment, another colorful Balinese idiom typically hurled at underprepared musicians is *batu malablab* (bah-too m' lub-*lub*). *Batu* means rock or stone, and *malablab* is the active form of the incisively onomatopoetic verb "to boil." A gamelan deserving of the sobriquet "boiling rock" is likely going nowhere fast.

The Balinese solfa syllables (scale tone naming system, see Chapter Three) are mellifluously based around changing vowel sounds within one word: *ding*, *dong*, *deng*, *dung* and *dang*. When pronounced in succession an extraordinarily clear harmonic line is created, one perhaps more evocative of an actual scale than the Western do, re, and mi. The syllables *dug* and *dag*, used to emulate certain Balinese drum strokes, might give rise to a series like *dug du' dug d' da dug da dug* when voiced in rapid succession imitating true drum patterns. With its random distribution of accents, this kind of phrase has been compared to the amusing spectacle of a chicken jerkily pecking on the ground for grains of rice. Associated with the same image is *nyog cag* (nyog-*chag*),[2] a term for a special style of rapid-fire

---

[2] Ruby Ornstein provided the *nyog cag* anecdote in her dissertation "Gamelan Gong Kebyar: The Development of a Balinese Musical Tradition" (UCLA, 1971) p. 227.

Colin McPhee (1900–1964), composer and ethnographer of Balinese music.

melodic ornamentation. If additional evidence of gamelan-like activity in the animal kingdom is required, anyone who has spent an evening in the Balinese countryside can attest to the polyphonic, rhythmic croaking of frogs in the rice-fields as being perhaps the most plentiful source of inspiration for local musicians.

Reflections in the natural environment and the thorough integration of gamelan into the communally based lifestyle of the Balinese provide a certain appeal that goes beyond pure considerations of sonic and structural beauty. Musicians everywhere seek recognition and reward for their art, but Bali is one of a handful of places in the world where there seems to be, at least at face value, a much greater overall respect granted to the role of music in sustaining the very foundations of society. We need not romanticize, as many have done, in order to discover the reality behind this assertion. Balinese musical culture will seem all the more remarkable after a sober assessment. Besides, the image of Bali as an idyll is a misleading oversimplification, as is the perception of the Balinese artist as a primitive living in an unchanging and perfect state of balance and harmony. In light of this, the achievement of Balinese music can be seen as a particularly extraordinary one. Perhaps this helps to explain the fascination that it has long held for foreigners.

International Reputation; Colin McPhee

A much-celebrated encounter between French composer Claude Debussy and the music of a Javanese court gamelan took place when a group from Java performed at the Paris International Exhibition in 1889. Debussy's works had already demonstrated certain characteristics akin to those of Javanese music, and his enthusiasm for the music he heard has generated ongoing debate amongst musicians as to whether his subsequent compositions specifically reflect the influence of the gamelan.[3] A complex question to answer, perhaps, but nonetheless a starting point for observing the slowly accelerating filtering of gamelan music into the consciousness of Western musicians and audiences.

The first Balinese group to tour abroad was the ensemble from Peliatan village, which played in Paris in 1931. A much more lavish and extensive tour by the same ensemble took place in 1952, organized by British entrepreneur John Coast. The group was a sensation in London, New York and Las Vegas and impressed the intricacies of Balinese music and dance on an international audience for the first time.

In the 1920s, the Odeon company released some recordings made in Bali. These came to the attention of Colin McPhee, a young Canadian-born composer living in New York. McPhee was an *enfant terrible* on the contemporary music stage of the time, possessed of the daring and idealism characteristic of the musical life of the era. He was immediately captivated by the recordings. The sounds of Balinese music awoke in him a singular ambition to hear the music at its source and to document it as fully as possible, setting aside (temporarily, he supposed) a promising career. He arrived on the island in 1931 and lived there more or less continuously until the forebodings of war necessitated his hasty departure some 8 years later.

McPhee arrived in Bali at a time of unbelievable musical activity. Village cultural life was aglow with creative freedom abetted by the ongoing decline of the courts and the shifting of artistic centers from the palaces to the banjars. He

---

[3] For an in-depth discussion of this issue, see Mueller, Richard "Javanese Influence in Debussy's *Fantaisie* and Beyond" in the Journal of Nineteenth Century Music, Fall 1986.

quickly mustered a retinue of friends, teachers and informants who helped him to realize his dream of a thorough record of the musical life of the era. A Steinway grand piano in the front room of his house in Sayan village was an object of delight for many Balinese, helping to make his home a favored meeting spot for well-known musicians. Working in tandem with Western colleagues such as anthropologist Margaret Mead and painter Walter Spies, McPhee became an expert on Balinese culture. His dedication and benevolence motivated him to act as a patron as well; he helped to reconstruct and revitalize many older styles of music in danger of extinction.

After his return home, McPhee never succeeded in recapturing the sense of inspiration and purpose that had been his while in Bali. During the subsequent period of his life he remained possessed by the charms of gamelan but found it difficult to communicate his enthusiasm to others, for whom the exotic remoteness of the island and its music remained a formidable barrier. McPhee's single acclaimed composition after 1930, *Tabuh-Tabuhan*, was a fantasia-like meditation for full Western orchestra based on Balinese musical ideas. Over the years the piece has been performed by major symphony orchestras throughout North America and Europe. He produced little or no notable new music after that, and found himself mostly in personal and financial hard times until towards the end of his life, when he accepted a professorship at the University of California at Los Angeles. Here he devoted his remaining years to scholarly pursuits and the establishing of a gamelan study program at the school.

McPhee's life ended in both triumph and tragedy. He died in 1964, only a few weeks after finishing his magnum opus, *Music in Bali* (Yale Univ. Press, New Haven, 1966), to this day the most exhaustive volume available on the subject in any language. He had been at work on it for over thirty years but did not live to see the final proofs. The book is a masterpiece of detail and organization that was quickly recognized as a classic in the fields of ethnography and music. Others have since researched Balinese gamelan—including many notable Balinese scholars—but all acknowledge a great debt to McPhee's thorough scholarship. The present book's modest ambitions would have been unrealizable without it.

Had he lived a few more years, Colin McPhee would have enjoyed more of the fruits of his labor. Appreciation of Balinese music has burgeoned internationally and its echoes can be heard resonating in the creations of contemporary composers throughout the world. In the footsteps of the Peliatan gamelan—with whom McPhee was closely associated—Balinese groups perform abroad constantly. His study group at UCLA became a model for similar groups worldwide. And as for McPhee's most ardent concern for the continued vitality of traditional Balinese music, he would have been gratified to learn that many of the rare styles for whose continued existence he feared have been preserved, in many cases as a direct consequence of his initial efforts.

Gambuh flutes and rebab, Batuan village.

CHAPTER TWO

A Brief History of the Music

EARLY in the first millennium A.D., a bronze-age technology emerged in Southeast Asia that ultimately facilitated the manufacture of musical instruments. The musicians of the Philippine *kulintang*, the *pi phat* of Thailand, and related ensembles in Myanmar, Cambodia and other places in that part of the continent all use bronze gongs in making music to this day. But it is in Java and neighboring Bali that the most development occurred, and it is exclusively these two places with which the term *gamelan* is associated.[1] In Java there are many independent traditions; best known among them are the exalted and complex musics of the Central Javanese courts Surakarta and Yogyakarta, and the more robust village gamelans of West Java (Sunda). These are but two of the many regions that sustain a rich repertoire there. Music in Java is a subject that has filled many volumes, but it is wholly outside the domain of the present book.

Balinese music ultimately traces its origins to Java, and even now the two islands' musics share similar instruments, tuning systems and general principles of organization. But beyond that, the music they each produce reflects the vast differences between their cultures and the temperaments of their peoples. Both are highly sophisticated, but while the courtly Javanese music is reflective, subdued, and wide open to the contributions of individual performers' lovingly crafted improvisations, Balinese music—especially that of the 20th century—is a juggernaut of brash and aggressive energy, deriving much of its effect from virtuoso ensemble coordination and dramatic contrasts in mood.

Bali and Java also share a history of monarchism and have benefited from the influence of the courts as patrons of the arts. Both maintain a strong attachment to the mythology of Hindu culture, which is especially remarkable in Java given the completion of its transition to Islam over 500 years ago. In Bali the limited geographic area and the native animism with which Hinduism combined served to insure the firm implantation of the gamelan tradition outside the palace walls as well, imbuing it with more of the visceral characteristics of a village music and allowing it to proliferate as a popular art even after the kingdoms crumbled and Indonesia asserted herself as a nation.

[1] The term is also found in Malaysia, but it refers to a different kind of ensemble which is rarely heard today.

Balinese music is first and foremost an oral tradition. While a kind of rudimentary musical notation does exist, it is rarely used. All music is passed down from generation to generation through the guru-disciple relationship. Musical style develops through the years in relation to changing public tastes and private patronages, the inspiration of creative musicians, and the general development of Balinese society.

The further back one reaches in time, the more difficult it is to be specific about the history of Balinese music. Scant information in the form of bas-reliefs (mostly at Borobudur and other sites in Java) and scattered *lontar* (palm leaf manuscripts) offer some clues as to what music may have been like during the middle of the first millennium A.D., when Hinduism swept through the Indonesian archipelago. The temple carvings depict instruments in use at the time, while the manuscripts generally offer more about the cosmological significance of musical activity than they do about the content and practice of the music itself.

The tale of a musical culture's development is always closely connected to the availability of technology and materials for building musical instruments. While bamboo, hardwoods and cowhide were always at hand for fashioning flutes, drums and simple keyed percussion instruments, it was the arrival of bronze culture from mainland Asia sometime prior to Hinduism that made the decisive difference for Javanese and Balinese music. As smiths learned to perfect techniques for casting gongs and later, forging slabs (keys), systems of tuning evolved, as did ways of combining the resulting instruments into ensembles.

One of the earliest Balinese ensembles for which written descriptions exist is the *gamelan gambuh*. It is mentioned in early lontar as the accompaniment to the Gambuh play, which portrays episodes in the life of the legendary Hindu-Javanese prince Panji. Still extant in Batuan village, Gianyar District, Pedungan near Denpasar, Depehe east of Singaraja, and a few other villages, this ensemble gives a good sense of the ancient origins of Balinese gamelan. The instruments represent what was probably state-of-the-art craftsmanship in the early centuries of our millennium.

Four deep-voiced bamboo *suling* (flutes) are the core of the gamelan. They are so long that, sitting cross-legged, a player must place the end of the suling on the ground some distance in front of him to be able to reach the mouthpiece properly. These suling, accompanied by the *rebab* bowed lute, spin airy, haunting melodies in a kind of fuzzy coordination that have a distinctive, ghostly sound.

The tuned metallophones so prominent in later Balinese gamelans were not yet being produced at that time. Instead, the percussion section of the orchestra is led by two high-pitched drums and filled out by a pair of small bronze gongs and a battery of indefinitely pitched bells, cymbals and chimes that underpin the melodies with a carpet of bright ringing accents. Altogether the effect is that of a music hovering in space restlessly; heard today it vividly evokes the bygone era that fostered it.

While certain sacred ensembles still heard in Bali today may in fact be older,

COLLECTION KITLV LEIDEN

Gambuh ensemble from North Bali, circa 1857.

the musical architecture of Gambuh melodies is a crucial precursor to nearly all Balinese music of the last several centuries. The musical principles and practices evident in gamelan gambuh compositions are still very much a part of modern Balinese music. The utilization of a firmly grounded core melody (here, the sulings and rebab), propelled onward and controlled for speed and dynamics by a pair of drums, and punctuated cyclically by gongs, comprise the backbone of most Balinese gamelans. That these techniques are so well-established in gambuh shows that they are quite ancient. The employment of gongs to delineate circular, repeating melodic cycles, particularly salient and pervasive in gamelan, is fundamentally opposed to Western music, which generally proceeds from beginning to end in a comparatively straight line. Some have suggested that the periodic and regenerative structures of gamelan melodies make an apt metaphor for the life, death, and reincarnation cycles so central to Balinese Hindu belief. Whether or not this connection can be academically substantiated, the analogy provides an apt description.

Music in the Courts

The spread of Islam throughout the archipelago during the 13th to 15th centuries steadily undermined the powerful Hindu Majapahit empire of East Java until its final collapse in the decades prior to the year 1500. This forced the royal entourages to take refuge on the Hindu stronghold of Bali. Their culture subsequently blended in with the existing Hindu/animistic beliefs of the native

I Ketut Maria (see Chapter Six) dances the Kebyar Duduk *during the nascent years of kebyar style.*

Balinese. The concurrent subjugation of local rulers, along with the formation of new kingdoms and a new social hierarchy, laid the foundation for a flowering of all Balinese arts. From that time until the arrival of the Dutch colonialists some four hundred years later, Balinese music blossomed in splendid isolation, producing a variety of forms, ensembles, and styles remarkable in their diversity.

The descendants of the Majapahit rulers, firmly ensconced in their royal palaces in what are now the eight *kabupaten* (regions) of Bali, were great patrons of music on the whole, and more often than not avid practitioners themselves. Gambuh was cultivated in the courts, as was the singing of lontar texts known as kidung and kekawin. With the advancement of bronze technology and the appearance of finely crafted gongs (to this day, though, the best of the large gongs are cast exclusively in Java) and metal keys, the bronze-based gamelan became prevalent in the courts and temples.

Musical accompaniment was *de rigueur* for an array of secular and sacred occasions of ritual, theater, and even just plain recreation. The famous sweetly-tuned *gamelan Semar Pegulingan* (from Semar, the god of love and *Pegulingan*, pillows room) played outside the king's bedchamber during afternoons of royal passion, using melodies ingeniously adapted from the gambuh repertoire for the full complement of bronze instruments. The enormous *gong gde* (great gong) orchestra, found today only in a few villages, accompanied ritual male dances and provided music for state and religious occasions—with a group of majestic instrumental compositions that to this day are heard in all temples at festival time. These dignified slow pieces, known as *lelambatan*, were nurtured during the post-Majapahit era and in many ways can be thought of as the soul of Balinese orchestral music.

The independent kingdoms, the talents and musical interests of their individual rulers, and their topographically necessitated isolation from one another, account for the great variation in musical styles that is in evidence today. For example, the *legong* dance and its music, which originated in the south-central courts of Sukawati and Blahbatuh during the late 19th century, quickly became popular throughout the surrounding areas, but made few inroads into the northern and western parts of the island. Those areas, however, maintained and continue to maintain special gamelans which to this day are still uniquely their own.

The Colonial Period

The Dutch encroachment into Bali was gradual during the 19th century and limited to the northern coastal regions. Then in 1906 they stormed southern Bali, resulting in the infamous *puputans* (mass ritual suicides) of the members of the Klungkung and Denpasar courts on the battlefield. These dramatic events helped to solidify Dutch control of the entire island, and soon a colonial administration was firmly in place. Though the Dutch were savvy enough to foster good relations with the kings when practicable, in effect the decline of the courts and their artistic patronages was at hand. Major cultural and social upheavals resulted when the musical traditions (and instruments!) that had heretofore been largely the domain of the higher castes were now passed down to the villagers.

The most significant musical event from the early part of the Dutch period was the birth of the *gamelan gong kebyar* in the villages of North Bali around 1915. This gamelan, a radical modernization of the standard temple orchestra, swept Bali in the following decades. *Kebyar* style became the *lingua franca* of Balinese music as no other type of orchestral repertoire had before. The high speed and capricious pyrotechnics of kebyar music are quintessentially 20th century in flavor, and bear the unmistakable stamp of a music at long last released from the precious refinery of aristocratic environs.

Up until kebyar completed this swift ascent, the *gamelan pelegongan* had reigned supreme. This orchestra, derived from the Semar Pegulingan but intended primarily for accompanying the refined legong dances, was at the time a fertile area for musical creation and experimentation. The great composer and teacher I Lotring of Kuta village, whose shadow towered over the island's musical world during this period, composed brilliant pieces and taught many village groups the subtleties of the style. His name is still mentioned today with reverence.

But soon villages were transforming their pelegongan gamelans into kebyars as fast as they could melt down the delicate bronze keys and recast them for the heavier, larger instruments of the new gamelan. The best-known teacher of kebyar from this period was Gede Manik of Jagaraga village in Kabupaten Buleleng. He zealously taught the dynamic new music—which he had helped to create—to villages all over the south, where it was embraced enthusiastically.

Once Lotring and his colleagues got their hands on the kebyar, however, they greatly enhanced the vocabulary of the music by imbuing it with some of the subtleties of pelegongan and other refined classical styles so deeply rooted in South Bali. It is in fact the flexibility of kebyar and its ability to adequately replicate the music of other gamelans that has accounted for its staying power. Even now in the north, though, purist groups continue to promulgate the undiluted, rough-edged original, to which they proudly lay claim.

Colin McPhee's presence in Bali during the 1930s resulted in his documentation of the awesome proliferation of musical activity in the villages during the colonial period. In addition to the types discussed herein, he covered many other styles that flourished—some sacred, some secular, some popular, some on the decline. With their new roles as successors to the custody of gamelan traditions, the village gamelan clubs and the teachers that led them brought about a great flowering of musical culture, effervescent with change and creativity.

Music Since Indonesian Independence

The years 1940-1965 were a time of war, liberation, revolution, political turmoil and even natural disaster in Bali. Gunung Agung erupted in 1962 just prior to an important ceremony at Besakih temple. The task of nation-building dominated the local scene much as it did throughout the new Republic of Indonesia. Inevitable responsibilities and conflicts made it difficult for Balinese to devote their energies to the arts as they had under the relative stability of colonial rule. But musical activity, albeit somewhat curtailed, did continue apace.

Gamelan gong kebyar, by now deeply entrenched in even the most remote villages, was so familiar that it was enough to simply use the word "gong" to refer to it. President Sukarno, himself part Balinese, was very fond of kebyar and often invited groups to perform at his behest in either Jakarta or at his Bali hideaway in Tampaksiring. At his suggestion a flurry of realist, nationalistically-oriented music and dance pieces were created during the early 1960s, but as this was at the opposite esthetic pole from the abstract, fantastical nature of most Balinese art, they did not find favor for long.

The obsession with kebyar was producing musicians of great technical skill. Their exuberance buoyed the music to ever increasing levels of speed and complexity. But at the same time, so much of the musical heritage—and the refined temperament embodied in the older styles—was suffering from neglect. This lamentable state of affairs was addressed in the early 1960s with the establishment of a High School and a College of the Performing Arts in Denpasar. Known as KOKAR and STSI (formerly ASTI, and still often referred to as such) respectively, these schools are part of a nationwide system that includes campuses around the archipelago. The faculty, drawn from the ranks of the best artists, were entrusted with the tasks of teaching, academic research, the active preservation of older styles, and the creation of new works.

The notion of imposing academic legitimacy on a music which had always thrived in its natural environment was at first viewed askance by some. After all, reasoned parents, why should I send my child to a school in Denpasar when there's plenty of music right here in our village? But as the reputation of the faculties grew and Indonesia adopted the standards of a global community which stresses the benefits of obtaining a degree, resistance lessened. Nowadays it is simply assumed that a serious young musician should get a formal education if he or she plans to earn an income from music. Yet KOKAR and STSI, because of the way in which they dominate the scene more than any individual village or court ever did, remain controversial.

Another important factor in the recent history of Balinese music is the advent of mass tourism. Many complain that musical standards tend to relax when a group performs for 'undiscerning' foreigners, but this notion is open to question and difficult to generalize about. Tourism is a kind of new patronage, and a great incentive for gamelans in tourist areas—both financially and in terms of civic pride. The Ubud/Peliatan district, for example, as anxious to preserve its reputation as a center for the arts as it is to sell tickets for nightly tourist shows, now boasts at least a dozen active ensembles. With the economic prosperity such villages enjoy, more gamelans are bought and more groups formed than ever before.

Even in villages off the beaten track, recent years have seen a renaissance of musical activity. Yearly government-sponsored island-wide gamelan competitions and the Bali Arts Festival, held every June and July in Denpasar, provide high profile performance opportunities for groups all over Bali. Newly established cassette companies compete for a growing market of consumers seeking good recordings of classical and modern gamelan music. A general sense of the importance of seeing traditional Balinese music through the tumultuous developments of our era is deeply felt by most. Most importantly, Balinese music is as essential for ceremonial and religious purposes as ever, and that state of affairs shows no signs of changing.

In the academies, and to some extent in the villages, the kebyar craze has peaked. Young composers are turning more and more to older types of gamelan for inspiration, while at the same time inventing musical techniques that stretch the boundaries of what is traditionally "correct". Only a musical culture very secure with itself could tolerate such experimentation. Moreover, interaction and collaboration with musicians from all over the world have become commonplace. This kind of cross-cultural fertilization is a natural development here, where valuable new ideas have always been accepted and cleverly transformed to meet the needs of the Balinese. It seems likely that the future of Balinese music is bright, even as gamelan musicians confront the array of new influences resulting from Bali's drastically expanded international profile.

Following pages: A gamelan foundry at the home of Pandé Made Gableran, Blahbatuh village.

Kempur and kemong, gamelan Semar Pegulingan, Ketewel village.

CHAPTER THREE

The Construction and Tuning of Instruments

PANDE Made Gableran's gamelan foundry, located just northeast of Blahbatuh village off the main road to Gianyar, is one of only a few such foundries in Bali. There is a group of smiths in the village of Tihingan, Klungkung, and one in North Bali at Sawan, southeast of Singaraja. The honorific *pande* precedes Gableran's name because as a metalsmith he belongs to the special Pande clan, an exclusive lineage that has been entrusted with the sacred responsibility of casting musical instruments and other important metal objects (such as krisses) for centuries. Among Balinese musicians Gableran is well known and trusted with the manufacture of many a new set of instruments and the maintenance and repair of old ones. He is a broker for the import and sale of large Javanese gongs and also for non-bronze instruments (such as drums) which are made in Bali but not assembled by his workers. He is heir to a rarefied art, a skillful technician, and a smart entrepreneur.

Gamelan instruments at all stages of production are in evidence during a walk through the interconnected courtyards of his compound. On the right, just beyond the entrance is the foundry proper. Scraps of *kerawang*, a bronze consisting of approximately three parts copper to ten parts tin, sit in small piles on pieces of banana trunk waiting to be weighed. The alloy is mixed here from raw materials, although it is considered better to reuse old kerawang when possible, such as may be obtained from instruments or other bronze objects broken beyond repair. Between one and two kilograms of metal is used per key or small gong, depending on the size of the instrument for which it is intended. Once the furnace at the rear is hot, the kerawang is melted at a searing temperature and fired for some time to insure a good blend. When it is removed, poured and allowed to solidify a bit, a gold vermillion form glows from within the mold. This is picked up very gingerly with tongs, forged into the proper shape with a hammer, and plunged into a basin of water. After it is cool enough to handle it is filed, scraped and polished until the lustrous surface of a finished key is recognizable.

In the back of the workshop, carpenters are splayed out amidst saws, chisels, lumber and shavings. The *pelawah* (instrument cases) are constructed here. *Ketewel* or *nangka* (wood of the jack fruit tree), a heavy and durable semi-hard-wood, is the preferred material, although other woods are sometimes used. Once

Instrument case carvers in Singapadu village.

the basic form of the pelawah is cut and assembled the carvers go to work, creating elaborate designs on every square centimeter of the wood's surface. Most patterns are standardized, featuring a pair of *bhomas* (earth gods) or *nagas* (serpents) watching vigilantly from each end with the edges and corners filled in with flowers and other elaborate patterns. These are completed quickly and somewhat nonchalantly by craftsmen who have the designs at the tips of their fingers. Imaginative and wealthy customers may request something a bit more complex, such as different scenes from the *Ramayana* or *Mahabharata* epics portrayed on each of a group of instruments, and as a result some gamelans are unique works of art. Once the carving is completed the wood is varnished or decorated with paint and gold leaf.

At the central pavilion the instruments are tuned and assembled. This requires expertise and a sensitive ear, and is entrusted only to Pande Gableran or one of his sons. If the instrument involved is a set of keys to be part of a gamelan gong kebyar, for example, and if no specific tuning is requested by the customer, the scale will be copied from a "family standard" set of keys that the tuner keeps beside him for reference.

The pitch of a key can be lowered by shaving some bronze from the underside, as this makes the key longer in proportion to its diminishing thickness and causes it to vibrate more slowly when struck. Filing along one of the ends shortens the key; consequently it vibrates more quickly and is higher in pitch. When the whole set is in tune, the keys are strung up in ascending order by looping twin strips of rawhide (or some sort of cord) through two holes that have been drilled, one at both ends of each key. The cord is secured with wooden pegs under each hole, and the whole set of keys is suspended over the pelawah by tautly tying the ends of the cords through eye hooks placed at either side of the wooden frame. The length of the cord is supported at intervals by little posts that act as trestles to keep each key freely suspended over its own bamboo resonator.

These bamboo tubes, snugly nestled into holes in the pelawah, must also be tuned so that the column of air that they support vibrates at the same rate as the key that hangs above it. The higher the pitch of the key, the shorter the resonating space needed. Bamboo grows in sections separated by nodes; Gableran cuts the tubes so that the space above the node leaves the proper length of air for its key. The section of bamboo below the node is non-functional. When viewed from the front, the nodes can be seen ascending from left to right like a staircase.

Balinese Tuning Systems

The standard that Gableran uses for tuning a gong kebyar (or any other type of gamelan) is unique to his family. Other Pandes have their own methods, as do many other craftsmen in Bali whose specialty is just to tune instruments, as distinct from casting the actual bronze. There is no agreed upon norm that would make all gamelans on the island compatible with each other. This ensures that each set of instruments has its own characteristic sound and tonal personality. How different this is from the way things work in Western music, where the frequency of the note A above middle C is universally agreed upon at 440 vibrations per second (or very close to it)! With all other tones adjusted in relation to 'A440', it is possible for musicians anywhere to play together with ease. Such a situation is simply not possible, nor even desirable, in Bali. What is more, since most Balinese instruments are percussive, it is difficult to adjust their tuning to each other without going through the elaborate procedure described above. But despite the role of individual taste in determining the sound of a set of gamelan instruments, there is yet a theory of tuning and scales in Bali.

Rather than think of Balinese tunings as scales, it is perhaps helpful to conceive of them as a set of guidelines for intervals (distance relationships between tones). This idea is flexibly interpreted by tuners, giving rise to the variety of tunings found in actual practice. Two sets of guidelines, or systems for tuning, exist. Both in Bali and Java they are commonly known by the names *pelog* and *slendro*.

Pelog is a seven-note system that, in Bali, originates with the *gamelan gambuh*. The notes are separated from each other by a series of unequal intervals. This is not as vague as it may sound, for there are generally accepted limitations as to how much the size of the intervals may vary. A crude "sample" pelog collection can be obtained on the piano by starting at E and progressing upward on the white keys to the next D. However, no Balinese pelog is quite as uniform as that!

In the gamelan gambuh and the gamelan Semar Pegulingan all 7 tones are present, but they are rarely all used during a single composition. Instead, groups of five are isolated to form modes, each of which are named. A given piece usually restricts itself to the five tones of its mode. Each of the five tones are labeled with one of the Balinese solfa names (similar to our *do, re, mi,* etc.) *ding, dong, deng, dung,* and *dang,* with *ding* considered to be the starting note of the mode. The chart below shows how the three modes *selisir, tembung* and *sunaren* are derived from the parent 7-tone Pelog.[1]

parent pelog tones:	1	2	3	4	5	6	7
selisir mode:	ding	dong	deng	(—)	dung	dang	(—)
tembung mode:	dung	dang	(—)	ding	dong	deng	(—)
sunaren mode:	(—)	dung	dang	(—)	ding	dong	deng

But gambuh and Semar Pegulingan are rare and ancient ensembles. Most pelog-tuned gamelans in Bali restrict themselves to tembung or selisir mode, both of which are distinguished by gaps after the tones deng and dang. (Sunaren is as well, but it is never mentioned as a source for tunings.) This combination of very wide intervals with comparatively narrow ones is responsible for the distinctive tonal character of most gamelans. No matter where the beginning of the mode lies in actual pitch—some gamelans may be higher, some lower—it is this succession of intervals which is its most identifiable feature. A possible selisir tuning on the piano could be played E-F-G-B-C; tembung could be played A-B-C-E-F.

The slendro system is inherently five tone.[2] It is found in the gamelan gender wayang used to accompany the shadow play and a few other ensembles. It also employs the ding-dong-deng-dung-dang syllabification of the tones. In contrast to the jagged, plaintive sound of the intervals in the 5-tone derivations of pelog, slendro is considered to be based on roughly equal intervals. Although in practice the distances between the tones are far from equivalent, slendro is nonetheless characterized by a smooth and harmonious progression. A very rough approximation of slendro could be played A-C-D-E-G.

With a little experience, novice listeners can learn to distinguish easily between the sounds of pelog and slendro, and also to appreciate the subtle differences between gamelans tuned in like systems. But there is an additional element in the tuning of any gamelan that is considered crucial, above and beyond the system or mode employed. It is the factor that gives gamelan music the pulsating, shimmering sound that travels so effortlessly through the evening air; the key to making the instruments 'come alive'.

---

[1] In his *Music in Bali* (Yale Univ. Press, 1966), McPhee also mentions the modes *baro* and *lebeng;* today these are considered archaic and mentioned only in connection with fingerings for flutes in gamelan gambuh. In addition, the sacred seven-tone ensembles gambang, selunding and luang make use of other mode classifications, which often vary from village to village.

[2] Some contend that it is another subset of Pelog, but this is an unusual point of view and difficult to substantiate.

In Western music, when pairs of like instruments, say clarinets, play a melody together on the same notes, we say that they are in unison. This means that they are producing sound waves of exactly the same dimensions, making for the simplest and purest concordance of sounds. The next purest would be at the interval of the octave, where one of the clarinets' sound waves moves exactly twice as fast as the other's. This 2:1 ratio is a kind of identity. We call a note that vibrates 880 times per second 'A' just like the one an octave below it, which moves at half that speed, or 440 vibrations per second. Sound waves traveling together in such simple mathematical relationships are perfectly synchronized and seem to our ears to be smooth and stable. In Balinese music, such tones would be considered wan and lifeless. Instead, pairs of instruments are intentionally tuned just slightly apart from one another so that when the same tone is struck on the two instruments simultaneously, the sound waves that emerge are of slightly different speeds. This causes an acoustical phenomenon called beating, which makes the tones seem agitated and charged with pulsations.

Most gamelans vibrate, or beat, at a rate of somewhere between 5 and 8 times per second, depending on the preference of the gamelan's tuner and the type of gamelan involved. In older styles of music the beating tends to be slower, but in modern ones the extra intensity of rapid oscillations is sought. In the case of a 7 vibration difference, every pair of instruments from the lowest to the highest must be tuned so that the one vibrates 7 fewer times per second than the other. This is no mean feat, because while that difference can account for a big discrepancy in pitch on the deep bass instruments, it may be barely discernible in the piercing upper registers. This is where the acute sensitivity of the tuner's ear really comes into play. Furthermore, in order to keep the rate of beating constant throughout the gamelan, octaves and other intervals within the scale must sometimes be compromised. But the result is fantastic—a glorious bouquet of tones each with its own character and relation to the whole. And when the full gamelan strikes up and a glistening cascade of sound rushes forth, the complexities of the tuning add a great deal to the intense visceral effect of the music.

Balinese Musical Instruments

The bronze instruments of the gamelan can be divided into two main groups: those with keys and those consisting of a gong or a group of gongs. Other types of instruments include barrel-shaped drums, bamboo flutes, cymbals, the bowed *rebab*, and a variety of other inventive music-making devices.

The keyed bronze metallophones in Balinese gamelans come in a number of different sizes and shapes and are struck with an assortment of different kinds of *panggul* (mallets). There are two basic structural designs for these instruments. Those in the *gender* family use bamboo resonators, above which the keys freely hang. In the *saron* (also called *gangsa jongkok*) family the keys are simply laid over a wooden trough, held in place with posts, and padded slightly with rubber where the bronze comes into contact with the wood. The sound is therefore much more

KANTILANS

PEMADE

UGAL

PEMADE

PEMADE

CENGCENG

KENDANG

CENGCENG KOPYAK

ONG KEBYAR

JEGOGANS

LUNG

CALUNG

GONG

KEMONG

KEMPUR

EMADE

PEMADE

REBAB

SULING

REYONG

KENDANG

ROMPONG

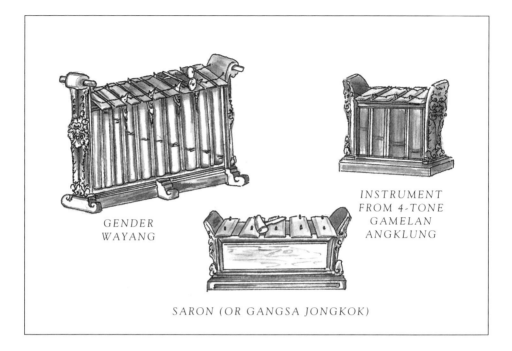

GENDER
WAYANG

INSTRUMENT
FROM 4-TONE
GAMELAN
ANGKLUNG

SARON (OR GANGSA JONGKOK)

crisp and brittle than the sound of a gender. Sarons are fairly uncommon in Bali, but they are found in a few ensembles. In Java their presence is quite standard.

A gender is classified and given a specific name according to several criteria, including the register of its keys, the panggul with which it is played, and the ensemble in which it is used. The deepest-toned instruments, usually with 5 keys, are called *jegogan*; they are played with a single padded mallet and emit long ringing tones. An octave higher in range and also 5-keyed are the *calungs*, sometimes called *jublags*. Another octave higher are the *penyacah*, but these are not always present. The function of this group of instruments is to play the core tones that form the basis for gamelan melody. They tend to play at a slower rate than the rest of the ensemble; in their sustained resonance the shimmering tuning of the orchestra is particularly audible.

The other group of gender in the gamelan are collectively known as *gangsas*. All are played with a hard wooden mallet and have from 7 to 12 keys, depending on the ensemble. These too come in three ranges. The largest and deepest, known as the *ugal* (or *giying*), is usually placed in the center. The ugal player sits on a high stool and leads the entire gangsa section. In the next octave are the 4 *pemade*, and above them, at the peak of the gamelan's range, are the 4 *kantilan*. The function of the pemades and kantilans is to flesh out the core melody tones sounded by the bass instruments with developed melodies and elaborate ornamentations.

The term *gender* proper is reserved for instruments that are played with two rounded wooden mallets, one in each hand. They are found in certain gamelans where the delicate tonal color they produce is required. Lastly, the miniature 4-

key gender-type metallophones of the gamelan angklung should be mentioned. Their melancholy tones can be heard at just about every temple in Bali whenever there is a ceremony.

The kinds of sounds that gender-type instruments are capable of producing are closely linked to the technique needed to play them. The lengthy resonances of the tones dictate that in any sequence of notes each tone must be stopped, or damped, either at the moment of or sometime before the arrival of the next one, in order to prevent the sounds from bleeding onto each other. For instruments played with a single mallet this is accomplished by grasping the key to be damped between the thumb and forefinger of the left hand. With two-mallet genders the fingertips and wrists are used. For slow passages these techniques merely require a little practice, but when the music gets fast—and does it get fast!—striking and damping motions follow each other in a wild blur of activity. But with the proper coordination and control the genders manage to emit a great range of sounds—from ear-splitting to nearly inaudible, and from silken smooth to biting staccato.

Gongs

The majestic gongs of Indonesia, and the technology for making them, form a central part of the archipelago's spiritual and cultural heritage. Particularly beautiful ones are prized as heirlooms, and are often thought to be the locus for strong magical and supernatural powers. In gamelans the gongs preside over the music like royalty at court, or like the heart over the mind and spirit.

Gongs used in Bali range in size from tiny high-pitched ones to enormous ones of 90 centimeters in diameter or more. With minor exceptions all are struck on the raised boss that protrudes from the middle of the gong's front surface; as with genders the deeper-toned ones require padded mallets. The smaller ones are hit with sticks wound with string for cushioning. Gongs aren't used or tuned in pairs the way keyed instruments are; the sound usually pulsates enough on its own to blend in well with the beating of the metallophones.

The most important function of the gongs in gamelan music is to mark structural points in a composition. The number of gongs employed for this purpose depends on the ensemble. Gong kebyar uses one or two *gong ageng* (the largest and deepest) for the beginnings and endings of melodies and other strong accents. If two, they are used in alternation and never together. Other divisions are the responsibility of the medium-sized *kempur*, the small, chiming *kemong*, and the nearly ever-present *kempli*, whose clear, dry sound taps out the steady beat on which all musicians depend when the rhythms get tricky. Other types of gamelans make use of some of these gongs, plus others like the tiny *kelenang*, the flat-bossed *kajar* and *bebende*, or a resonant version of the kempli called *tawa-tawa*.

Sets of 8 to 14 small gongs, arranged in ascending order of pitch and balanced on taut cords strung along a long wooden frame, are used in a melodic role. When such a set is played by a soloist it is called a *trompong*; when played by four people (each commandeering only a few of the gongs) it is called *reyong*.

The former is known for its sophisticated melodic style and is usually associated with older ceremonial music. The reyong, mainly a 20th century development, is known for its dizzying ornamentations and 8-note brassy chords, formed by having each of the four players strike a gong with each hand. An older version of the reyong, in the gamelan gong gde, requires only four gongs and two players.

No survey of bronze instruments would be complete without mention of the ubiquitous cymbals called *cengceng*. The enormous *cengceng kopyak* come in pairs and are similar to Western crash cymbals in manner of sound production. They are played in groups of at least four pairs, most often in ceremonial and processional gamelans. Most cengceng, though, are smaller and come in sets of six or more. All but two are set on a wooden base and struck by the unmounted ones, which are held by the player. The rapid-fire rhythms that result are an essential component of most any gamelan performance.

Drums and Other Instruments

Most gamelans are directed by a pair of *kendang* (drums). These are usually made of nangka wood shaped into a tapering cylinder and hollowed out in the middle in an hourglass shape. Skins are affixed at both ends by means of a long rawhide strip laced back and forth between the heads in an N-pattern, and tightened with sliding rings to control the tension on the heads. Kendang vary in size; the smaller the drum the more delicate the style of music with which it is associated.

Kendang are held across the lap and played on both heads with the fingers and hands, although sometimes a panggul is used in the right hand. In each pair the higher-pitched one is designated the *lanang* (male), and the lower-pitched the *wadon* (female).[3] The drums produce a variety of sounds (each named with the usual flair for onomatopoetic syllables)—like *kap, pak, dag, tut, pung* and so on—and an intricate technique for playing them has evolved. Often overpowered by the rich textures of the gamelan melodies they support, the rhythms of the Balinese kendang are in fact the motor that drives the orchestra.

Many instruments popular in Bali are made solely of bamboo tubes strung up in wooden frames. Such instruments are light, inexpensive, relatively easy to make, and are usually associated with recreational rather than ritual music. The most often encountered ones are known variously as *tingklik, grantang* or *rindik*. They are the sort of instruments that people keep around the house to fool around on, but they are often combined into larger ensembles as well. Rice farmers are said to have invented them as a way to keep idle fingers busy while resting in some shady spot away from the midday sun. Visitors to Bali often hear tingklik performed as background music in hotels and restaurants. Yet despite these casual associations, there is a rich repertoire of music for them.

Balinese *suling* (flutes) are universally made of bamboo. They are end blown from a nodal point in the tube, with a little hole cut in to allow the breath to

---

[3] This apparent reversal of male and female voice characteristics has never been satisfactorily explained to the author!

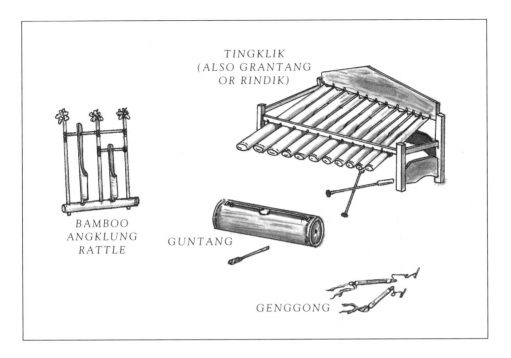

TINGKLIK
(ALSO GRANTANG
OR RINDIK)

BAMBOO
ANGKLUNG
RATTLE

GUNTANG

GENGGONG

pass through the resonating chamber. Fingering holes are bored along the length of the instrument. The husky *suling gambuh* is the longest, with all sizes available down to a piercing little one that can be heard through the texture of the loudest orchestral passages. Suling are always played with circular breathing, a difficult technique whereby the flutist exhales air stored in the cheeks while inhaling through the nose. This makes it possible for the flute to sound continuously.

The instruments described above are the most frequently encountered in Bali, but the list is far from complete. Bali is peppered with all sorts of unusual music-making tools. The bowed *rebab*, already mentioned in connection with gamelan gambuh (see Chapter Two), finds its way into many ceremonial ensembles. It is much loved for the dignified tone it imparts when well-played. The sound of a poorly played rebab, though, has been compared by some Balinese to the squeals of a pig being slaughtered at feast time!

Other instruments include the *genggong* (a jew's harp), the *guntang*, (a sort of gong made from bamboo fashioned as a slit drum), the *preret* (a reedy trumpet heard in East Bali and Lombok), and many other ingenious devices made from simple and readily available materials. The panoply of Balinese musical instruments runs the gamut from the sophisticated construction of the gongs and metallophones down to such simple objects as a piece of bamboo and a stick. All find their way into the world of Balinese music.

Small suling (bamboo flutes) are both sweet and shrill, and can cut through the loudest gamelan sonorities.

CHAPTER FOUR

Basic Principles of Gamelan Music

TO investigate the way that a music works is to uncover the manner in which the musicians and composers in a particular tradition express themselves and their culture. At their disposal is their own creative power, consideration of the uses to which the music will be put, and the possibilities suggested by the musical instruments that they possess. They are bounded by the limits of their experience and what their culture accepts or deems artistically suitable. The act of composing music is the act of ordering and patterning the flow of time; hence the way that the musicians in a society choose to do this says quite a lot about their philosophical perspective and aesthetic outlook.

In much of Western music, time is conceived of as linear. A composition begins, proceeds, its themes are elaborated upon, and it ends, all in a continuously unfolding process. While certain melodies or sections may be repeated during the course of a work, they are just as likely to return in a changed form as not. This is part of what makes the music challenging and satisfying to follow. The Western musical aesthetic, in turn, might be correlated with wider cultural notions about progress, development and change.

In Balinese gamelan, as in many other musics throughout the world, it is more accurate to characterize musical time as cyclical or regenerative. That is to say the music normally returns repeatedly to the same 'point', like a planet in orbit or the hands on a clock. Perhaps, as was suggested in Chapter Two, this reflects the importance of reincarnation in Hindu belief, or possibly it symbolizes an attachment to the ever-replenishing harvest cycles that have supported agriculture on Bali's soil for centuries. In any case, most sections of a gamelan composition are strengthened through immediate and literal repetition. This is achieved in such a way that the last note of a melody is also the first note of its recurrence, as though a circle was being drawn and the final arc closed. That moment of renewal is of primary importance and is signified by a stroke of the large gong.

The circular temporal distance that passes between two gong strokes is filled in with a variety of melodies and rhythms. Perhaps the most important of these is the slow, measured line of the 5-keyed calungs, stressed occasionally by the deep-toned jegogans, which comprise the 'core' melody. All other aspects of the music—the rhythmic variations, shifts in tempo and intensity, and the impressionistic changes of color—owe their allegiance to this basic tune, which can be heard sailing placidly through the middle and lower registers of the ensemble. Other elements in the music may transform rapidly and unpredictably, but the core melody and the gong are the dependable safeguards of cyclical time.

Since the music is orchestral in conception it follows that there are many different musical parts. Each part is related in a specific way to the core melody and the gong and can be derived from or traced to them with ease by an experienced musician. The different kinds of musical parts do not vary very much between pieces and are usually executed by the same groups of instruments. Thus every instrument in the ensemble has a precisely prescribed role to play in making up the whole—a fleshing out of the musical curve carved out between the soundings of the gong, and a richly detailed set of variations on that single, core melodic line.

In our description of gamelan music it will be helpful to divide the instruments of the ensemble into two groups—those that play the core melody or some sort of variation on it, and those that describe the melody's form or shape. Thus the former group, consisting of the jegogans, calungs, gangsas, suling, rebab, trompong and reyong (in short, all of the tuned instruments) provide the melodic content of the music. The latter group, headed by the large gong and including its smaller siblings the kempur and kemong, the time-beater kempli (or kajar), the cengceng, and the two kendang, furnish a framework for the melody. Every instrument in the gamelan, like every person in Bali's structurally complex society, has a crucial role to play.

Instruments that Trace the Form

Just about all gamelan music is grounded by a large gong to mark the beginnings and endings of melodies and a kempli or kajar to keep a steady beat. Musicians are so dependent on the reassuring sound of these two instruments that if their players are ever absent from a rehearsal confusion is bound to ensue. In between the strokes of the large gong, the smaller gongs find their places—different places depending on the type of melody. The form of the melody is therefore delineated by 1) the number of kempli beats between two strokes of the large gong, and 2) the particular pattern of strokes of the lesser gongs. This technique of using gongs to define the form has been dubbed *colotomy* (from the Greek *colon*, meaning arm or limb) by Western musicologists; the arrangement of gongs within a melody is referred to as the *colotomic structure*.

Colotomic structures range in length from 2 kempli beats to broad canvasses of 256. In general the shorter the pattern the more it is repeated within a composition. The warm sound of the kempur and the contrasting sharp peal of the kemong, appearing within the cycle at crucial points, furnish a set of musical signs that enhance the power of the return to gong. They are almost always placed in such a way as to divide the cycle into even sections of 2, 4, 8, 16, or 32 beats. The sense of expectation engendered by such equal time divisions makes the arrival of the final gong a very satisfying event, especially after one of the longer patterns.

Playing the kempli is a skill that requires admittedly little instrumental dexterity, yet it demands a complete and thorough understanding of the music and an awareness of fine shadings of tempo. The beat of the kempli sustains and coordinates the ensemble, scouting out upcoming changes in speed and adjusting the beat accordingly without rocking the boat too much. Musicians unconsciously look to it to fit their rhythms into place. In rare instances where the ensemble's coordination threatens to unravel, the players' eyes and ears will hone in immediately on the kempli's beat seeking clarification, and the kempli player is expected to provide it in no uncertain terms.

To get a feeling for one of the most characteristic colotomic structures, try studying, and then singing or clapping, the 16-beat phrase notated below at a comfortable speed. The key underneath explains the symbols and sounds used. This pattern is known as *gegaboran*; it is found underlying melodies in a variety of female dances related to the offering dance *gabor*, and also in instrumental music.

GONGS:	G				P				M				P				G
KEMPLI:	K	K	K	K	K	K	K	K	K	K	K	K	K	K	K	K
BEAT #:	1	2	3	4	5	6	7	8	9	10	11	12	13	14	15	16 (1)
SING:	*Gir*	*tuk*	*tuk*	*tuk*	**Pur**	*tuk*	*tuk*	*tuk*	**Mong**	*tuk*	*tuk*	*tuk*	**Pur**	*tuk*	*tuk*	*tuk* **Gir**

Key:	Name	Symbol	Sung Syllable and Pronunciation
	Gong	G	**Gir** (*sung on a low pitch, like English 'gear' with a rolled 'r'*)
	Kempur	P	**Pur** (*sung on a medium pitch, like English 'poor' with a rolled 'r'*)
	Kemong	M	**Mong** (*sung on a high pitch to rhyme with English 'long'*)
	Kempli	K	**Tuk** (*half-sung with a nasal sound, like English 'took'*)

(The 'tuk' sound is dropped if it coincides with one of the other gongs.)

There are a wealth of different colotomic structures used in Balinese music. Most conjure up a specific connotation for Balinese listeners, not unlike the way major and minor scales carry emotional associations in Western music. The gegaboran form noted above, for example, will always bring with it the affect of a delicate female dance, even if it supports a melody for a purely abstract and

The two kendang control the ensemble, the kempli monitors the tempo, the ugal carries the lead melody.

instrumental composition. Likewise there are gong patterns that tend to call forth warlike sentiments, regal splendor, spiritual refinement and other responses. These feelings are further enhanced and modified by several factors, including the note of the scale with which the stroke of the large gong coincides, the tunings of the gongs in relation to the gamelan's scale (some gamelans' gongs match one of the pitches in its scale, others' fall completely outside of it), and the tuning of the gamelan as a whole.

The Core Melody and its Variants

The core melody and its variants fit snugly into the colotomic structure. The tuned instruments each have their own parts, organized in levels so that the higher the pitch of the instrument the more complex the music it is called upon to play. In this stratified arrangement very stately sustained tones are relegated to the jegogans, a singing midrange line (the core melody itself) is played by the calungs, the ugal and the trompong play a developed version of the calung part, and the rest of the instruments fill the upper register with a shower of high speed ornamental figuration called *kotekan*. This arrangement is often metaphorically compared with a tree, where the core melody is represented by the trunk, the ugal and trompong by the limbs and branches, and the kotekan by the flowers or leaves. As with the colotomic structure, the relationship between the parts is based on even multiples. The kotekan instruments move 4 or 8 times faster than the calungs and the ugal, which in turn play 2, 4, or 8 times faster than the

When playing kotekan, the musicians' mallets move up and down in coordinated alternation.

jegogans. The busy chattering of the kotekan is solidly supported by the mellifluous tones and booming gongs below it.

Usually, the core melody is sounded by the calungs at the rate of one tone per one or two kempli beats, although sometimes, especially in contemporary music, it is given more shape and not restricted to such a uniform rhythm. The jegogans are similarly regular, stressing the important notes of the calung line by simply doubling them on their keys, which sound an octave below. The jegogans also unfailingly coincide with the gongs, as if anchoring the core melody to the foundation provided by the colotomic instruments. At the ends of melodies, when the large gong, jegogans and calungs all play together, the resultant sound, enhanced by the gamelan's paired tuning, is very physical in its effect. Playing in the group or listening close by, the vibrations can be felt as well as heard.

The core melody is usually too plain in itself to be particularly tuneful; its function is to proceed dependably like a sturdy walking bass in a jazz combo. In the registers above it, its tones are ornamented by the numerous melody instruments that it supports. The most flowing, singable version of the core melody tones—the ones a Balinese would sing if asked for their version of the 'main' melody of a given piece—is often buried in the middle of the texture on the tones of the ugal. This role falls also to the elegant trompong in older pieces; there it is much more prominent. Ugal and trompong each have their own distinctive style for ornamenting the core melody tones, connecting them to each other with syncopated curves and graceful melodic loops that always end up just where they should when final gong arrives.

Since the ugal and the trompong are generally not paired, and are therefore not coordinated note-for-note with any other musicians, their players are allowed some flexibility in interpreting the melody. This flexibility imparts a certain sense of fluidity and openness to the music. The skill with which these parts are executed greatly affects the feeling for the rest of the ensemble, so these instruments are entrusted to players of great skill. Their roles are among the few places where improvisation, albeit within a narrow range, can play a role in Balinese music. The suling and rebab, when present, also interpret the core melody in an improvisatory style, adding a much-desired sweetness of tone. But their presence is optional, whereas the music cannot possibly be played properly without the ugal, and in some cases the trompong.

Kotekan

The busy upper registers of the gamelan are the domain of the gangsas and reyong. These instruments spin out kotekan, the crackling ornamental fireworks of Balinese music. Kotekan is usually expressed in English as 'interlocking parts', because although it sounds as one melody it is actually composed of two interdependent musical lines that are incomplete when played alone and dependent exclusively on each other for obtaining the desired result. That can range from stately murmuring in some of the older, simpler styles of kotekan, to extroverted, jazzy acrobatics in modern music. The tight interaction of the two parts produces a supple texture that is pointillistic in detail and fluid as a whole.

The two components of kotekan are termed *polos* and *sangsih*. The polos is derived from the core melody and coincides with it from time to time, while the sangsih complements the polos by filling in any rhythmic gaps in its structure. From the two parts' interaction, a motoric steady stream of melody emerges. In some kinds of kotekan this means that the polos simply plays a regular succession of two notes per kempli beat. The sangsih interlocks with this by playing right in-between the polos tones; together they divide the beat into four equal parts. In other kinds both polos and sangsih are composed of syncopated rhythms which complement each other ingeniously. In such cases the two parts occasionally coincide at the unison or some sonorous interval. This produces irregular accents that bubble up from the flow of the kotekan's melody, dancing skittishly around the smooth beat of the kempli. Much of the excitement of Balinese music arises from these irresistible rhythms.

A very common and straightforward kind of kotekan is called *nuutin*, which means 'following' in Balinese. In it, the polos rests comfortably on the same tones as the core melody, striking twice per beat and moving to a new note only when the core melody does. The sangsih fits in between, repeating the next-highest tone in the scale. The result, diagrammed below, is like a slow trill or rocking back-and-forth between the two parts. In performance one can see the polos and sangsih players' mallets moving up and down in coordinated alternation.

Sangsih tones:		S	S	S	S	S	S	S	S	
Polos tones:	P	P	P	P	P	P	P	P		
Calung tones:	C	–	–	–	–	–	–	C	– – – – – – –	*etc.*
Jegogan tones:	J	–	–	–	–	–	–	–	– – – – – – –	
Kempli beat:	K		K		K		K			

A more syncopated type of kotekan, in which the polos and sangsih coincide every few notes, could be represented like this:

Sangsih tones:		S S	S S S	S	S S	S S	
Polos tones:	P	P P	P	P P P	P P	P P	
Calung tones:	C	– – –	– – –	– C	– – –	– – –	*etc.*
Jegogan tones:	J	– – –	– – –	– –	– – –	– – –	
Kempli beat:	K		K		K		K

Notice that in both examples every part of the beat is filled with either a polos or sangsih tone, or both.[1]

An enormous variety of kotekans have been created and new ones are being invented all the time. They provide endless beguilement for gamelan musicians and are a showcase for the talents of their composers. But too much complexity is wearing for the listener, so kotekan is not employed exclusively. Sometimes the upper registers ring out with bold and strikingly profiled unison passages that provide welcome contrast—and give the players' tired hands a break! Moreover, kotekan is most effective at quick tempos, where the rhythmic excitement finds its most comfortable gait. At slow speeds, languid melodies often weave through the texture. Sometimes it is slow enough for both parts of the kotekan to be handled by a single player; this imbues the patterns with an entirely different, more relaxed character. A balanced diet of slow and fast, some kotekan and some unison passages, is considered essential in any piece.

But playing kotekan at the unimaginable speeds that some gamelans attain requires terrific coordination, a flawless instrumental technique, and musicality sensitive enough to respond to the precise, unmistakable 'click' of polos and sangsih settling into their complimentary rhythmic niches. The sensation of being locked in with another part, racing through a melody in a breathless rhythmic embrace, is an epiphany unlike any other musical experience in the world.

Role of the Drums

The two kendang that direct the gamelan play elaborate patterns that are like kotekan. The higher pitched *lanang* (see page 38) is roughly comparable to the polos—its rhythms generally align with those of the kempli. The deeper *wadon's*

---

[1] In the next chapter, a complete kotekan pattern will be discussed in detail.

A good trompong player can communicate the richness of the lelambatan repertoire.

part is composed to fall in between. Together they produce phrases that move at or near the speed of the kotekans. In addition to negotiating these complexities, one of the drummers is also responsible for coordinating the entire gamelan's changes of speed and volume, for interpreting any cues that a dancer may give, and for signalling the beginnings and endings of sections.[2] For these reasons among others, the kendang is considered to be the most difficult instrument in the gamelan. This is partly because of the dexterity, endurance and strength required to master the technique of playing, but also because a drummer must understand all aspects of the music and know all of the other parts exhaustively in order to be a competent director. Almost invariably drummers lead rehearsals and create new compositions too, making their role especially seminal.

In certain kinds of music, notably some of the male dance forms, the music moves too swiftly and the changes come too abruptly for participation by a pair of drummers to be practical. In such cases the lead kendang player takes over alone and plays in a virtuosic, improvisatory manner. The repertoire of rhythmic patterns on which to improvise is broad and drummers delight in collecting them, inventing them and putting them together in different combinations. The best players develop a very personal style over the course of their careers, acquir-

[2] Whether it is the wadon or the lanang that fulfills this function depends on the type of music. In the gamelan gong kebyar the wadon is usually the leader, but for certain music, notably the male dance forms and masked dances, the lanang takes over. The lanang also has a primary role in the older styles gambuh, Semar Pegulingan and pelegongan.

ing signature phrases and rhythmic tricks that are designed to baffle would-be emulators and give a distinctive mark to their playing.

Perhaps the highest compliment that a drummer can receive is that his playing is *suba ela*—that is, completely natural and easy, despite the intricacies of the rhythms. The best kebyar drummers 'dance' while they play, using their torsos, arms, hands and facial expressions to help express the music, show the degree to which they have mastered it, and to add drama to the performance. In older styles of music, a more reserved demeanor is considered appropriate.

The experience of performing on the lead kendang in a Balinese gamelan is one of exhilaration and responsibility. All members of the group seek clarification and reassurance that the music is proceeding as it should by listening carefully for important drum cues and by establishing eye contact with the drummer when possible. The drummer must be fluent enough with his part that most of his energy can be directed towards monitoring the group, constantly checking to make sure that things don't go awry. If there is a dancer, the kendang acts as intermediary, translating key dance movements into musical impulses with deftly placed strokes that send messages in a flash to the ensemble. The drummer communicates the essence of the music in sound, bearing and gesture.

Tempo, Dynamics, and Other Subtleties

Balinese musicians speak of *laya*, or ensemble feeling, as a fundamental aspect of any performance. Executing the core melody, gong strokes, melodic variations and drum patterns with mere correctness is only the first step in playing a piece of music. Any group worth its salt must also master the spirit and nuance of a composition, knowing just when to speed up or slow down, when to get loud and when to get soft, and whether to do so suddenly or gradually. The music and the musicians must breathe together.

The prime aesthetic criterion for a good gamelan performance is that of tight ensemble coordination. In order to achieve this every part is carefully composed, memorized, and then practiced again and again until its execution is a matter of reflex and instinct. Consequently, with the exception of the few very limited cases described above, there is virtually no improvisation in Balinese music. The goal is instead to achieve complete mastery of a given piece of music and to play it to perfection together with the rest of the ensemble. While playing, each musician listens attentively and is aware not only of his or her individual part, complex as it may be, but also of its relationship to the whole and especially to the core melody. Soloists emerge rarely; instead each member of the gamelan tries to be precisely coordinated with the others, like a vital part of a single living organism.

Change of tempo originates with the signals of the ugal and kendang players and is regulated by the careful increase or decrease in the rate of kempli strokes, all of which must be alertly followed by the rest of the group. Plenty of practice is needed to perfect the suspenseful, gradual accelerations and ritardandos that are such a hallmark of the music. The effect of 25 or more musicians changing speed in perfect synchronization is very impressive indeed, especially when one takes into account the difficulty of keeping kotekan rhythms interlocked even at a steady pace! Sometimes, notably at transition points or endings, the tempo leaps to a higher or lower level very suddenly. In such cases, the players must memorize the sensation of playing at both tempi and be able to switch from one to the other with ease.

There is great sensitivity to gradations of loud and soft in Balinese music. The wide dynamic capacity of the instruments is thoroughly exploited with both subtle and violent changes in volume. Often extremes of dynamic are juxtaposed to create an atmosphere of tension and unpredictability. Cues for such changes are given by the ugal player, who indicates the dynamic of an upcoming passage by raising his mallet. The higher it goes, the louder the subsequent section will be. These changes are never decided extemporaneously, however, but are planned at rehearsals and specified note-for-note.

Laya also finds expression in the palette of tonal colors available and through the contrasts that are achieved by bringing out the sound of a particular group of instruments. A repeating melody may be enlivened by having the gangsas play louder than the rest for a few cycles, followed perhaps by turns for the suling, kendang, calungs and reyong. The spectrum of sound shifts gradually as one group fades out and another emerges. Sometimes a section of the gamelan drops out altogether for a time, revealing a sparser, more translucent texture.

Often the steady flow of drums, melody and kotekan is rocked by a sharp, syncopated accent called *angsel*. This term originates with the dance, where it refers to a sudden and unexpected movement which is mimicked in like rhythm by the gamelan. But angsels are a crucial agent for rhythmic variety in instrumental music too. They are always preceded by a few beats with cues from the kendang and ugal. At the right moment—usually just prior to the gong—the kendang, cengceng, gangsas and reyong converge on the angsel rhythm. But the gongs and core melody continue ineluctably, undisturbed by the commotion around them.

Form and Composition

Musical form in Balinese music runs the gamut from short pieces made up of a single repeating melody to multi-movement works of symphonic breadth and scope. In older music, the form is determined by the colotomic structure—that is, a piece of music is classified and named according to the pattern of gongs marking it. Modern pieces may be freer and more fantasia-like, concatenating a succession of rhapsodic melodies, or even introducing passages that involve no colotomic punctuation at all.

Ostinatos (short, repeating melodies) are important in processional music and for accompanying many male dance forms. They also appear as stirring finales to lengthy ceremonial pieces and in any dance or theatrical setting where a brisk, martial mood is appropriate. By far the most common colotomic pattern for ostinatos is the *gilak*, an 8, 16 or 32-beat structure that features two kempur

The form of the music is delineated by the pattern of gong strokes.

strokes aligned towards the end of the cycle in a peculiarly asymmetrical way. They seem to make the music fall headlong into the gong that follows, as if pulled in by gravitational forces. If the gamelan has one, a second large gong, somewhat smaller than the main one but still weighty enough in sound to contribute substantial power, is used to mark the middle of the cycle. The 8-beat gilak, with large gongs on beats 1 and 5 and kempur on beats 6 and 8, can be notated as follows:

Gongs & Kempur:	G				G	P		P	G	
Kempli beats:	K	K	K	K	K	K	K	K	K	etc.
Beat #:	1	2	3	4	5	6	7	8	1	

Listen for the dense pulsations of gilak in the *gamelan bebonangan*, the ensemble of gongs, kendang and cengceng used in processions. The urgent excitement it generates adds a great deal to the atmosphere at such occasions. Other important ostinatos encountered in Balinese music are the aforementioned *gegaboran*, associated with female dances, the *bapang*, used in *jauk* and other choreographies, and the *batel*, common in dramatic contexts for accompanying fight scenes.

At the other end of the spectrum are the majestic long forms that comprise the heart of the classical repertoire. In the temple at ceremony time, one gamelan usually holds forth with *lelambatan* (lit: slow music) for the pleasure of the visiting deities. Here Balinese music reaches its zenith of structural development with long and convoluted compositions that take up to 45 minutes to perform. Adapted from the repertoire of the gamelan gong gede of the courts, these pieces are distinguished by the presence of the trompong and the boom of kendang played with mallets; they are also accompanied by the constant clash of the giant cengceng kopyak. The sheer weightiness of the sound of lelambatan gives a good indication of its significance.

A lelambatan usually opens with an austere and meditative introduction for trompong (suling and rebab are often present as well), punctuated sparely with pulsating jegogan tones. The rich resonances of the trompong's tones and the graceful melodic ornaments supplied by the player reach deep into the melody, bringing forth a wealth of musical feeling. Soon the drums enter and, following quickly, the rest of the gamelan. The ensuing phrases explore a variety of textures and tempi, often previewing melodic ideas that are slated for a role later on. After a time the trompong and drums emerge again, heralding the *pengawak*, or main movement.

There are 8 varieties of lelambatan pengawak, named and distinguished from each other by their length and colotomic structure. The simplest is *tabuh pisan* (*tabuh* = composition; *pisan* = one), which usually consists of eight melodic phrases of 16 beats, bisected and finished with strokes of the large gong. Other types of lelambatan pengawak form involve the kempur and also the kempli, whose role is altered from that of beat-keeper. Among them, *tabuh kutus* (*kutus* = 8) is the broadest. Here, kempli and kempur strokes alternate, separated from each other by 16 beat phrases, until each has sounded eight times. When gong finally arrives, 256 beats have elapsed—a considerable time and musical distance (see diagram below).

```
————————————— P          —————————————
————————————— K          —————————————
————————————— P          —————————————
————————————— K          ————————————— G
————————————— P          —————————————
————————————— K          —————————————
————————————— P          —————————————
————————————— K          —————————————
————————————— P          ————————————— G
————————————— K
————————————— P          Form for tabuh pisan (1) pengawak
————————————— K
————————————— P
————————————— K
————————————— P
————————————— K
————————————— P          Key:   K = Kempli
————————————— G                 P = Kempur
                                G = Gong
Form for tabuh kutus (8) pengawak    Each line = 16 beats
```

Form for tabuh kutus (8) pengawak

Form for tabuh pisan (1) pengawak

Key: K = Kempli
       P = Kempur
       G = Gong
       Each line = 16 beats

Many compositions exist for each of the forms, and while the melodies are always different and there is some flexibility as to how the totality is constructed, the colotomic structure and drumming patterns for the pengawak section are constant from piece to piece. Individual lelambatan are referred to by their pengawak type and a given name. For instance, *tabuh nem Galang Kangin* (*nem* = 6) means "Eastern Sunlight: type six lelambatan composition".

The pengawak is majestic in tempo and may be repeated 3 or 4 times in a temple performance. Often the atmosphere in the temple is so informal that the musicians take coffee and cigarette breaks between repetitions! Actually they are in a kind of holding pattern, waiting for indications that the ceremony is about to intensify. When the flow of offerings being carried to and from the inner courtyards is bustling and the priests begin chanting the sacred ceremonial rites, the trompong player cues the musicians on to a series of other movements which build slowly in speed and excitement while growing proportionately shorter in length. This telescoping of musical energy is timed to synchronize with the progress of the rituals. Usually by the final section the scope of the composition has been reduced to that of an ostinato, which brings the piece to a thundering conclusion. As the tones of the lelambatan fade away they are supplanted by other sonic activity: the sweet-toned gamelan angklung (which often plays right across the courtyard), groups of women singing ancient songs, loudspeaker announcements, the barking of vendors on the street outside, and the gossamer tinkling of the high priests' bells.

Lelambatan melodies are subtle and restrained, using mainly simpler types of ornament and kotekan. What may at first seem to be a rather flat and monotonous texture reveals itself upon repeated listening to be a rich trove of inventiveness and Balinese musical feeling. These are the pieces closest to the hearts of most Balinese. They hear them regularly in the temple from childhood on, and associate their dignified demeanor with the rarefied spiritual world that they encounter there.

Other Ensembles, Other Forms

In the compositions that comprise the repertoire of the ancient gamelan gambuh and its direct descendants gamelan Semar Pegulingan and gamelan pelegongan, a variety of musical forms have evolved. Many of the colotomic structures used resemble those in lelambatan, but in these delicate styles the large gong is replaced by the kempur and the kempur defers to the bright sound of the kemong. In really authentic versions, the flat-bossed kajar unseats the kempli, tapping along in tandem with the patter of the small kendang used rather than simply stating the beat. A suite of melodies for the legong, the much-beloved series of classical Balinese choreographies for young girls, opens with a lengthy prelude—the dance of the *condong*, or court attendant. The condong's dance is based on 4 ostinatos that are interspersed and repeated with variations in tempo, ornamentation, and angsel. Thereupon follows a medium-sized pengawak and a number of shorter movements arranged according to the particular legong story portrayed. It has recently become acceptable to omit some of the longer melodies in performances of legong in order to shorten the performance; hopefully this will not diminish appreciation of the complete versions, which are magnificent compositions and should be preserved in full.

Musical structures in other kinds of gamelans are faithful to the basic principles of cyclical structure and core melody with variations, but they vary greatly within that context. Compositions for the gamelan gender wayang may be associated with specific scenes or characters in the shadow play or underpin the puppeteer's singing. The instrumental pieces for this gamelan are jewels of labyrinthine melodies and kotekans. The 4-tone gamelan angklung that is often heard in the temples makes the most of its tiny range with its own special kotekan style, nestled into colotomic patterns of often odd and unpredictable lengths. The bamboo-keyed gamelan joged bumbung and gamelan jegog, tremendously popular in the western part of the island, adapt some of their music from popular songs.

A few older gamelans with wholly sacred uses base the formal structure of some pieces on verse forms in classical poetry. The number of lines in the poem and the number of syllables in each line are used to determine the number of phrases in the melody and the number of beats in each phrase. Further, the vowel sounds used in the poetry can actually be mapped on to the musical phrase to construct the melody itself: a, e, i, o and u in the text become *dang, deng, ding, dong,* and *dung* in the music!

Most of these gamelans have fixed repertoires that are tampered with only a little today, if at all. The 20th century has seen revolutionary changes in Balinese musical form, however. These had their beginnings in the 20s and 30s with the works of Lotring and his contemporaries. Lotring had a genius for constructing free-form works for the pelegongan and kebyar gamelans that vividly evoked other Balinese styles. His compositions *Gambangan* and *Angklungan* (based on the musics of the gamelan gambang and the gamelan angklung) lifted those styles out of their restricted ritual settings and made use of their melodies and rhythms in a secular, non-functional context. Lotring was especially expert at gamelan gender wayang. He modified many pieces from this style, transposing them from their original slendro into the pelog tuning that was his preferred compositional medium.

Lotring's work opened the door for other composers to rearrange, invent, alter and discard musical ideas and materials as it suited them, as long as the music they composed was intended for secular use. The sacred styles, then as now, remain intact. The *kreasi baru* (lit: new creations) music and dance compositions for the gamelan gong kebyar that appeared by the hundreds during the following decades were freely composed, eclectic and novel, often emphasizing the virtuosity of the musicians and flashy new styles of kotekan. By the late 1970s, though, this excess of freedom had been allowed to degenerate into cliché.

Composers today have recognized this and are remedying the situation in several ways. One is by refining the existing kreasi baru style. Another is to return to composing in older forms. A third way has been to invent new instrumental techniques and combinations or even new instruments. This last group has produced some brilliant and intriguing new ideas. Komang Astita, a young musician from Denpasar, composed *Eka Dasa Rudra*, using several gamelans at once to evoke the cacophony of the massive centennial ceremony of the same name that was held at Besakih temple in 1979. Other composers have playfully used such objects as kitchen utensils, rocks and brooms in their whimsical and energetic recent work.

There are few limits on what is acceptable or possible in Balinese music today. The accelerated pace of life on the island is reflected in the broadening of what the culture as a whole accepts as artistically viable. Composers and their music are as susceptible to these changes as any other segment of the society; this naturally has resulted in the rapid development of untried and unusual musical forms. Most of these will not have any impact beyond the excitement of their initial performances, but a few will stick. Recent music reflects the new approaches to aesthetics and the new artistic liberties that are part of Balinese life now.

The drummer mediates between dancer and gamelan by being watchful and alert to cues.

CHAPTER FIVE

The Music for
the *Baris* Dance

INITIAL encounters with music as foreign to Western ears as Balinese gamelan are understandably bewildering to most. Even for sensitive and sympathetic listeners it is difficult to make much sense of the music until after repeated exposure to the new sounds, instruments and tunings. The problem is compounded by the fact that the music is orchestral and so much is happening at once. Some sort of step-by-step guide that applies the abstract concepts presented in the previous chapter to a particular piece of music therefore seems worth pursuing.[1]

The strategy will be to coach you in understanding, singing and playing all the different parts for one short composition, using the same sounds and syllables that a Balinese musician would if they were not playing on the actual instruments. Our tools will be the four notes *do, mi, fa, sol* (skipping *re*) of the Western major scale, a steady foot tap or hand clap, a robust (and not necessarily beautiful) singing voice, and a little time and patience. Those with greater musical aptitude may do better on the complex ornamentations than others, but do not let this daunt you. All of the parts are important and a facility with any of them will reward you with increased appreciation of the music. If you are in Bali, ask a musician to help you if you can. He or she may well be delighted by your interest.

The discussion will be limited to a detailed description of the music for the *Baris* dance, as played on the standard gamelan gong kebyar tuned to 5-tone pelog. The modern solo Baris is a dance form with its roots in antiquity. The word itself means row, rank or file and actually refers to a whole family of choreographies that portray martial and warlike characters. Most of these were originally for companies of dancers bearing lances or shields; the group forms still extant today are mainly sacred and seen only at special ceremonies. The solo dance, however, has been distilled and secularized. Today it can be seen on the program at many recreational performances, whether as entertainment for Balinese outside a temple during a ceremony or as part of a tourist show.

---

[1] The contents of this chapter are coordinated with the Baris selections on a CD that is available from the School of Music, University of British Columbia (see back cover for details).

While the older ritual Baris forms are comprised of relatively plain choreographies, the execution of the more intricate modern one requires intensive practice and consummate skill. Most male and many female dance students begin their training with this dance, as it develops the most important musculature, movements and postures in the Balinese dance vocabulary. Since the dancer may in effect vary the order of the larger gestures of the choreography during the course of a performance, a Baris performer must have complete understanding of the musical accompaniment too, as he is required to instantiate these gestures at precisely the proper moment in the course of the music. In contemporary Baris the dancer leads the gamelan, carrying the musicians along through a succession of sharply drawn moods and vignettes that illustrate the warrior's alternately watchful and combative states.

Beryl De Zoete and Walter Spies, writing in *Dance and Drama in Bali* (Faber and Faber Ltd., London, 1938, p. 168), give the following evocative description of the Baris' character: "The evolutions of this dance can be of intense brilliance: the fierce darting glance, the neck movements so swift that they seem like a trill of sound; the leaps, the wheeling flight; the restless splendour of glittering crest and swinging stoles; ... the sudden smile, infinitely alluring; the narrowed eyelids lifted to reveal blazing balls of darkness set in a shining rim. Sometimes a lightning pirouette will lift in a whirl of color the short brilliant stoles which hang thick as feathers on his back. The Baris dance has an undeniable fighting bird quality."

Baris is usually 10 to 12 minutes long. The music and the dance are in three parts, each of which are based on 8-beat colotomic structures. The first and last parts are quite similar to each other, while the central section is wholly unrelated. We shall concern ourselves with the first part only. The intent is to give as complete a picture as possible of what is happening in the music and how it is connected to the dance through words, diagrams, notations and photographs.

Before we proceed, a pair of disclaimers. Baris has been chosen for our purposes because it is one of the most ubiquitous pieces of music in Bali. In spite of the brevity of its melody it contains all of the elements found in more developed pieces. But because it is so common there is also regional variation in performing it, so that the version discussed in the following pages may differ a bit from the one you chance to hear in performance or on a recording. These discrepancies, however, can only be at the level of minor detail; the various parts set forth herein will unquestionably be identifiable as parts of Baris to any Balinese, even though they may not coincide exactly with the way it is performed in his or her village.

Secondly, there is the matter of tempo. Baris, like much Balinese music, is played impossibly fast. Attempting to follow music moving at such breakneck speeds can be very frustrating since it requires a vigilant and unwavering concentration as well as a thorough familiarity with the materials, especially when it comes to the kotekan and kendang parts. Practice what is given here slowly until you can execute it well, but prepare for a shock when you listen again to a performance. The musicians will invariably play faster than you can think! Of course, the players themselves are *not* thinking, rather they are repeating gestures that they have practiced together thousands of times. After awhile you will be able to follow them. In the meantime, imagine the thrill of doing something so fast and complex in coordination with so many others.

Our notation will be simple. The Balinese solfa syllables (see page 32) will be used to indicate the tones in the melodic parts. In the notations beginning on page 62, each musical line will be written across the page and shown above and in relation to the pattern of gongs and kempli in the cycle. Next to each notation will be a sketch of the instrument that it is played on, with the specific gongs or keys used in Baris darkened in.

A word about the configuration of gongs and keys on the instruments: we have seen that *ding, dong, deng, dung* and *dang* of a five-tone pelog tuning can be roughly compared to our *mi, fa, sol, ti do,* or E-F-G-B-C. In the gamelan they are extended over a range of more than four octaves, with the tones divided amongst the instruments (in most instances) as shown below:

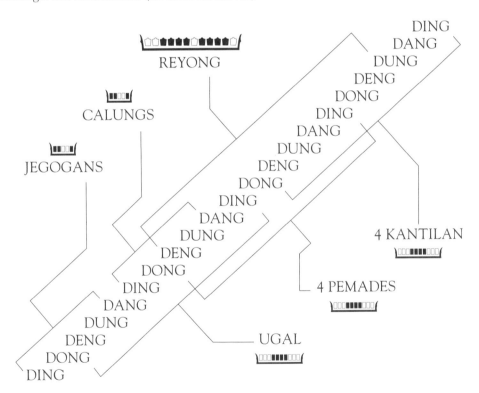

In addition to having different ranges, it is evident that the instruments also have individual arrangements of keys or gongs. The jegogans and calungs cover only one octave, beginning on *ding* and ending on *dang.* The ugal, pemades and kantilans, separated from each other by octaves, each begin on *dong* and stretch up ten notes to high *ding.* The span of the twelve gongs, or pots, of the reyong connects midrange *deng* with *dung* more than two octaves above. Hence, if all the players strike the note *deng* together, the calungs and jegogans will hit their 3rd key, the gangsas their 2nd (or 7th), and the 1st, 6th and 11th reyong pots will be played. Tunes that roam the full two octave range of the gangsas must be rearranged in order to squeeze the core tones into the single octave of the calungs and jegogans. Thus even though it sometimes looks as though players' mallets are moving in opposite directions, they may actually be playing the same notes.

Introduction and Form

Baris opens with an arresting kendang fanfare, usually performed solo in a fairly improvisatory style by the lead drummer playing on the higher-pitched lanang drum. The slapping sound produced by the left hand is called "*pak*," and the deep pitch obtained from striking the right drumhead with a mallet is called "*dug*" (say: doog). Both may be used freely in a few declamatory opening phrases, but after a moment the following rhythm emerges, instantly recognized as a cue by the ensemble.

pak DUG pak DUG pak DUG DUG DUG DUG DUG DUG *BYONG!*

The last group of six even "dug" strokes sets the tempo to come, one kempli beat for every two "dugs." Led by the raised mallet of the ugal player, the entire gamelan comes crashing down on the note *dang* right after the final drum stroke, making an explosive attack the Balinese call "*byong*." After a few flourishes the large gong sounds, the kempli starts tapping the beat, the jegogans and calungs enter, and the Baris melody proper begins.

The Baris ostinato is in gilak form (see page 50). From the sounding of the initial gong, the colotomic instruments and core melody cycle continuously until the end.[2] Meanwhile, the rest of the instruments may be said to be in either a "poised" or an "active" state. In the former they are repeating prescribed patterns. In the latter they are somehow reacting to angsels—signals given by the dancer—by interrupting the flow of those patterns. The poised state is quiet, static and tense; the active state is explosive and kinetic. Moving from the former to the latter is a matter of sudden release and violent crescendo. When the dancer completes the angsel movement the activated instruments simply drop out and remain silent for a moment, leaving only the colotomic instruments, jegogans, and calungs. Soon they reenter on their patterns as before.

Simple Melodic Parts

Once the introduction is over and the dancer has entered, we can count on the music to remain in the poised state for a few moments. This is a good time to focus on the various melodic parts. Don't attempt to hear all of them at once. Choose one and search for it in the texture with your ears. When you are

[2] There is one point at which the core melody does change; this will be taken up later.

Ritual baris dancers, North Bali, circa 1857.

satisfied that you have found it and can understand its relationship to the kempli and the gongs, move on to another part.

The most easily discernible melodic part is the tune played on the ugal and doubled both one and two octaves higher by the 4 pemades and 4 kantilans. Of the ten keys available on these instruments, the melody uses only numbers 4, 5,

6, and 7. (Refer to the diagram on page 59.) These are the notes *dang, ding, dong,* and *deng* (On the piano: C, E, F and G/*do, mi, fa, sol*). In singing, however, the Balinese tend to replace the hard "d" sound with "n" or "nd," Hence *dang, ding, dong, deng* becomes *nang, ning, nong, neng.* The ugal part has a simple one tone per kempli beat relationship to the colotomic pattern.

The colotomic notation for the gilak, with the beats numbered 1 through 8 is the foundation upon which we shall lay the ugal part (and all the other parts in turn). The pitch "*nang*" should be used for gong and "*neng*" for kempur, but the syllables remain, as described in the previous chapter, "*gir*" for gong and "*pur*" for kempur. The "*tuk*" sound used for kempli need not have a specific pitch. The notation for the ugal and gongs is given below.

		neng							
UGAL:		nong		nong	nong			*etc.*	
			ning				ning		
	nang				nang		nang		
KEMPLI:	K	K	K	K	K	K	K	K	K
GONG & KEMPUR:	G				G	P		P	G
BEAT #:	1	2	3	4	5	6	7	8	1

In the pemades' and kantilans' version there are two mallet strokes per kempli beat. The melody is identical to the ugal's, with one small deviation— half of the players replace the note nang with neng whenever it occurs, as their coincidence creates a harmonious sound. This may be difficult to hear, but it does enrich the sound at those points. On the other pitches all play together.

	nengneng		nengneng	nengneng		neng		
PEMADES & KANTILANS:	nongnong		nongnong	nongnong		*etc.*		
		ningning			ningning			
	nangnang			nangnang		nang		
KEMPLI:	K	K	K	K	K	K	K	K	K
GONG & KEMPUR:	G			G	P		P	G	
BEAT #:	1	2	3	4	5	6	7	8	1

Next, the core melody itself. It comprises every other ugal tone beginning with the arrival of gong, except that the note on beat 7 is lowered to *ning* to give the line a smoother curve. Observe that because of the calung's limited 5-note range, we must choose a different configuration of keys. Instead of *nang* being the lowest note used, it is now the highest. This is simply because no other choice for that tone is available. In singing the line, raise *nang* one octave from the position it had earlier.

		nang				nong				nang	
CALUNGS:				ning				ning			
KEMPLI:	K	K	K	K	K	K	K	K	K		*etc.*
GONG & KEMPUR:	G				G	P		P	G		
BEAT #:	1	2	3	4	5	6	7	8	1		

The jegogans are an octave deeper than the calungs and play half as fast. As it turns out, the jegogans play together with the large gongs in Baris. Their slow rocking between *nang* and *nong* is like an axis on which the music turns. The order of the keys is identical to the calungs'.

		nang				nong				nang	
JEGOGANS:											
KEMPLI:	K	K	K	K	K	K	K	K	K		*etc.*
GONG & KEMPUR:	G				G	P		P	G		
BEAT #:	1	2	3	4	5	6	7	8	1		

Reyong Kotekan

After you are able to hear and identify these four parts, try to memorize them. If you have internalized the core melody and these simple variations on it, it will be much easier to relate them to the kotekan and drumming, which we shall take up next. When practicing these more complex parts, proceed slowly and break the line up into as many sub-units as necessary to facilitate your learning. Keep a steady beat with your foot or a hand clap, and always be aware of the connection between it and what you sing.

Recall first that kotekan consists of two interlocking parts, polos and sangsih, which fit together to make a single composite line. The resultant sequence of notes occurs at a rate of 4 tones per kempli beat, for a total of 32 in the complete Baris cycle. To clarify this in our notation, each kempli beat has been calibrated into four equal divisions. The interlocking parts for Baris are composed in such a

Beats	:	1	.	.	.	2	.	.	.	3	.	.	.
Reyong/Sangsih	:	ne'	neng		neng			ne'					
			no'		no'		nong		nong				
				ning		ning	ni'		n				
Reyong/Polos	:	nang	na'		na'			nang					
Ugal (*main melody*)	:	nang			nong			ning					
Calung (*core melody*)	:	nang						ning					
Kempli	:	K			K			K					
Gong & Kempur	:	G											
Kendang Lanang L H	:												
R H	:		dug	du' dug	dug		dug	dug					
Kendang Wadon L H	:												
R H	:	dag	dag		dag	dag		dag	d				

Notation of reyong and kendang parts, with gong, kempur, kempli and calungs (core melody).

Beats (Clap)	:	1	.	.	.	2	.	.	.	3	.	.	.

Reyong/Polos : nang – na' ning – na' ning – ni' nang – n
(*Key:* na' nang = do; ni', ning = mi)

Singing the reyong polos part alone

Beats (Clap)	:	1	.	.	.	2	.	.	.	3	.	.	.

Reyong/Sangsih : ne' no' neng – no' neng – nong – ne' nong
(*Key:* no', nong = fa; ne', neng = sol)

Singing the reyong sangsih part alone

Beats (Clap)	:	1	.	.	.	2	.	.	.	3	.	.	.

Kendang : dag dug dag du' dug dag dug dag dug dag dug d

Singing the composite drum part (for one person)

| 4 | . | . | . | 5 | . | . | . | 6 | . | . | . | 7 | . | . | . | 8 | . | . | . | 1 |

ne'   neng   ne'   ne'   ne'   ne'   ne'   neng

   no'   no'   nong   nong   nong   nong   nong

      ning   ni'   ni'   ni'   ni'   ni'   *etc.*

nang   na'   nang   nang   nang   nang   nang   nang

neng   nong   nang   nong   ning   nang

     nong   ning   nang

K   K   K   K   K   K

     G   P   P   G   *etc.*

     pak   pak pak   pak pak

dug   dug   dug   dug   dug

      kap   kap kap   kap kap

da' dag   dag   dag   dag   dag

| 4 | . | . | . | 5 | . | . | . | 6 | . | . | . | 7 | . | . | . | 8 | . | . | . | 1 |

nang – na' ning – nang – ni' nang – ni' nang – ni' nang – ni' nang – ni' nang *etc.*

| 4 | . | . | . | 5 | . | . | . | 6 | . | . | . | 7 | . | . | . | 8 | . | . | . | 1 |

ne' no' neng – no' ne' nong – ne' nong – ne' nong – ne' nong – ne' nong – ne' *etc.*

| 4 | . | . | . | 5 | . | . | . | 6 | . | . | . | 7 | . | . | . | 8 | . | . | . | 1 |

dug da' dag dug dag pak kap dug dag pak kap pak kap dug dag pak kap pak kap dug dag *etc.*

Baris dancer: seledet (eye movement).

way that there is little regularity in the way they fall amongst these divisions. Sometimes they coincide with the kempli strokes and other times they avoid them entirely. Because of these irregularities, it will be difficult to grasp the kotekan parts unless the four subdivisions of the beat are clearly demarcated in your mind's ear. They should tick along steadily like a little internal stopwatch.

The Baris kotekan is assigned to the four reyong players. Players 1 and 3 handle the polos, which is played entirely on the notes dang and ding (pots number 3-4 and 8-9 for players 1 and 3 respectively), while the sangsih, naturally, is the responsibility of the other two musicians and is played on the tones *dong* and *deng* (gongs 5-6 and 10-11). The remaining pots are not used. This configuration is diagrammed on pages 64-65.

Polos and sangsih are composed so that every note in their patterns lasts for either 1 subdivision (1/4 beat) or 1 subdivision plus 1 subdivision of rest (1/2 beat). The interlocking occurs when one part sounds one of its tones at each instant that the other part is resting. This is how the continuous flow of notes is created.

To sing the parts, Balinese cut the final "ng" of the syllables when the kotekan note lasts for only 1/4 beat. In other words, *nang, ning, nong* and *neng* sometimes become "na," "ni," "no," and "ne." Practice and memorize both parts, together with a friend if possible, This way when you know them you will be able to work on making them interlock together.

Notice further that the kotekan tones that coincide with the kempli are in all cases the same as the ugal part at those points. It might therefore be said that the ugal tune is 'imbedded' in the kotekan, with the rest of the notes acting as decoration. Indeed, this is what is meant when the kotekan is referred to as ornamentation of the main melody. Observe also that the outer notes nang and neng always sound together. In performance this means that the polos players' left hands and the sangsih players' right hands are synchronized. The interlocking can really be 'seen' in the interaction between the inner notes ning and nong, which are never struck at the same time. The coincidence of the outer tones, however, produces accents which emerge from the running line of the kotekan each time they are sounded, creating the aural sensation of an independent and irregular level of rhythm protruding from the texture. As you listen to the reyong in performance, try to zero in on this phenomenon. For an additional challenge, try to isolate those points of accent from the kotekan and sing them alone while tapping the beat.

Kendang Patterns

There are two different but closely related kendang patterns composed for Baris. One is used when the dancer is stationary or moving slowly, the other is for when the dancer steps briskly around the stage. The second one is given below the reyong notation on pages 64-65; it uses a greater variety of rhythms. The first, simpler one, will be derived from it presently.

As we noted when describing the kendang introduction to Baris, the higher-pitched lead kendang produces the sounds "*pak*" and "*dug*" with the left and right hands respectively. The former sounds like the dry crack of a whip and the latter, played with the mallet, a resonant bass. The deeper secondary drum requires the same technique to produce sounds that are equivalent but lower in pitch. On this drum "*pak*" is called "*kap*" and "*dug*" becomes "*dag*." Kap, pak, dug, and dag are the only four drum sounds used in Baris.

The kendang's interlocking is conceptually similar to the reyong kotekan: one part fills in when the other rests. Unlike the reyong, though, the drum patterns never coincide. Instead, like sounds interact successively with like sounds, resulting in lightning combinations like "*kapakapak*" and "*dadugdadug*." (In singing quickly, as with kotekan, final consonants may be dropped.) When the dynamic is soft, the composite rhythm of the kendangs sounds like a vague and expectant rumble, but when the music gets loud the swift exchanges crack and boom like thunder.

As with the kotekan, it is best to practice the drum parts with a friend in order to get the effect of the interlocking. In addition to singing them, try using the more percussive sounds obtained by substituting a handclap for dag and dug and a slap of the chest or thigh for kap and pak. As you build up to the complete pattern try working on just beats 1-4, repeating them cyclically. Just this much, played twice to fill a full eight-beat cycle, is the other, simpler, Baris kendang pattern mentioned above. Its resultant should sound as follows, with claps taking

PREPARING
ANGSEL LANTANG

PREPARING
ANGSEL BAWAK

EXECUTING
THE ANGSEL

FINISHING
THE ANGSEL

Baris dancers' angsel movements.

the place of *dag* and *dug* syllables as given.

—A—

🮇. PLAYER 1:   dug   du' dug   dug   dug   dug   dug   dug

🮇. PLAYER 2: dag   dag   dag   dag   dag   dag   da' dag   dag

—B—

⬭ KEMPLI: K   K   K   K   K   *etc.*

BEAT # :   1   2   3   4   1 (or 5)

Pay close attention to the "double" *dag* and *dug* strokes marked A and B above. These are the only places where the regular one-to-one alternation of strokes between the kendang is disturbed. The effect is to make the drums exchange positions with respect to the kempli beat, thereby adding extra energy and syncopation to the music. This also makes the patterns tougher to play, however, so persevere. Take consolation in the fact that many Balinese drummers spend the better part of their lives perfecting Baris patterns.

We have now described what most of the instruments in the gamelan are doing while the Baris melody is in its "poised" state. The only exceptions have been the suling which essentially follows the ugal melody, and the cengceng, which play at the same rate as the drums and reyong, lining every subdivision of the beat with a sparkling metallic edge. The cengceng part can be sung 'ch-k-ch-k-ch-k-ch-k' using a breathy and dry quality of voice.

Interaction With the Dance

All of the ways in which the music and dance move between poised and active states involve communications which originate with the dancer and are interpreted sonically by the lead kendang. Some dance movements like the *seledet* (a quick flicking of the eyes to the extreme left or right and then back to center) are answered by the drums and cengceng alone. In other more developed angsels, the whole gamelan gets into the act.

With preparatory gestures the dancer signals what he is about to do and the lead drummer, fluent in the language of the dance, knows precisely how and when to react to it. It is the prerogative of the dancer to initialize such movements as he sees fit, but his precise choice is limited by the structure of the music. That is, he must always begin and end the angsel at places predetermined in relation to the colotomic structure. This means that the dancer must be as conversant with the music as the lead drummer is with the dance.

The seledet and other small movements of the head and/or upper body alone are echoed instantaneously by a crisp "*pak*" stroke or two from the kendang. These can occur at a few different places within the cycle; most often they fall immediately after the 7th beat. Since the rest of the gamelan is not involved, the lead drummer need only abandon his normal part for a moment to deliver the required accent and then resume it as before at the next repetition of the melody.

The full angsels are of two types: *bawak* (short) and *lantang* (long). In the former, the dancer dramatically lifts his bearing about halfway through the cycle. The lead kendang reacts just before gong with a series of right hand accents—*dug du'dug!*—that shatter the hushed and tense poise of the ensemble. Led by the ugal, the rest of the players explode into action at the arrival of gong, playing their parts at peak intensity. The dancer lunges and pivots and, for a few exhilarating seconds he, the drummers and the ensemble are coordinated in a terrible rush of energy.

Then, before we can even expel our breath, the dancer finds his footing and the reyong, gangsas, kendangs and cengceng come to an abrupt halt. There are a few beats of repose as the core melody and gongs are revealed, an inexorable current flowing beneath the vicissitudes of the dance. A final, biting "*kap-pak*" from the drummers' interlocking left hand strokes puts an emphatic period on the sentence. At gong the rest of the gamelan enters as before, ready to renew the process at the whim of the dancer a few cycles hence. The full angsel bawak process is diagrammed below, showing the interaction of the dancer and musicians in relation to the kempli beat. The entire process takes two full cycles.

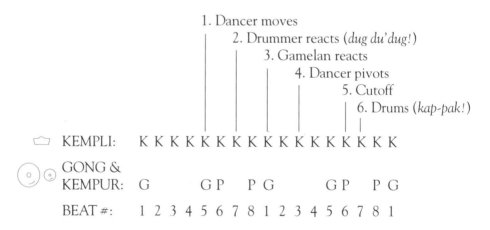

The angsel lantang, as the name implies, is longer and also more complex than the angsel bawak. It is initiated when the dancer assumes a curious half-stooped position, as though preparing to spring upwards, immediately after an angsel bawak. The kendang answer with a special cue and at gong the gamelan responds with a crashing accent, just as it did before. Except that this time the core melody changes, causing the gangsas to leap into the higher registers and the kotekan to change too. Only the gilak form outlined by the gongs and kempli is constant. This dynamic and unexpected disruption is the climax of the performance. For several cycles the dancer and the gamelan swoop and soar through alternating passages of loud and soft, release and tension, movement and restraint. At last the dancer concludes the angsel by initiating another angsel bawak. As the gamelan follows, the melody returns to its former position and the music resumes as before.

Although it is true that the ordering of the angsels is at the dancer's discretion, in practice this turns out to be not entirely the case. Most dancers and gamelans that work together regularly establish a more or less set choreography that varies but little from performance to performance. This usually consists of a relatively static opening that builds to several angsel bawak and one angsel lantang. Up to this point, the dancer has used only a part of the stage. During the next section, movement is much freer as the dancer traces the perimeter of the space, in the process interpolating many angsel bawak. The cue for the second angsel lantang is also the cue for the imminent ending. Following the angsel, the lead kendang gives a signal which communicates instructions for the final repetition of the cycle, which is in a slower, more cadential tempo.

What has been explicated above is only the first of the three large sections in a Baris performance. The second one, which follows immediately, is called the bapang. It has a different structure and is itself divided into three parts which share a single core melody but are distinguished from each other by their tempi: fast, slow, fast. The final part of Baris returns to the gilak.

Following pages: *Gamelan luang, a rare and sacred type of gamelan maintained in Singapadu village.*

Gamelan gambang, a sacred ensemble, playing at a cremation in Ubud.

CHAPTER SIX

Ensembles and Repertoire

BALI has developed and nourished an astonishing variety of musical ensembles—a kaleidoscope of sound and rhythm all the more remarkable because of the island's tiny size. There are more than two dozen distinct species of gamelan, each with an established tradition, repertoire, and social or religious context. Some, like the gamelan gong kebyar, are to be found by the hundreds all over the island, from the most isolated mountain hamlets to the crowded neighborhoods of Denpasar. Some are less common but thrive nevertheless, like the intimate chamber music of the shadow play's gamelan gender wayang. Others are strange, often sacred anomalies found in only a few villages or temples, particularly in the lush eastern and northeastern hills.

It is almost sufficient to point to the creative vigor and experimental predilections of the Balinese as an explanation for this diversity. Certainly no other place in the world, large or small, has proportionately as much or as many kinds of music in it as Bali does, and this happy state of affairs can only be attributed to the efforts of the Balinese themselves. But other more concrete factors have always been present to provide a context for such elusive variables as artistic temperament to assert themselves. One of those crucial elements is the topography of the island. Bali is sliced north/south by a network of deep ravines that, until the modern era, severely limited interaction between denizens of even closely situated villages. As a result, many styles of music developed in relative isolation from one another.

Economics and patronage have played important roles, too. In the past, some gamelans found nurturance exclusively in the courts, either because they were massive and hence beyond the financial reach of the villages, or else because their esthetic qualities were too refined to earn a meaningful place in the lives of any but the leisure class. Still, the musicians employed in the courts were commonfolk, and the musical education they received at work was put to good use at home supplementing the established grassroots traditions. Aristocratic styles of music frequently took hold outside the palace walls, often transformed and adapted for less ostentatious bamboo instruments. Many kinds of bamboo ensembles also have their own histories, and plenty of enthusiasts in communities all over Bali. But even in such villages, there has never been an adequate substitute for the powerful sound and aura of a bronze gamelan, in particular the large gongs at the heart of them. Few communities would deign to entertain visiting deities without one.

Repertoire in Balinese music was entirely dependent on ensemble and context until the 20th century. Every piece of music was associated with a specific type of gamelan and intended for a rigidly prescribed occasion. Sacred music was for use only in the temples and music for entertainment was kept out in no uncertain terms. To have suggested otherwise would have been tantamount to heresy. Today these restrictions have been relaxed somewhat and many sacred compositions have found their way into secular life, often in transformation form and adapted for recreational gamelans (although this process does not go in the reverse direction). This does not necessarily lessen the music's ritual power, though, because when such pieces are played in the sanctum sanctorum an entirely different set of standards continues to apply—one wholly indifferent to life outside the temple.

One could fill volumes with just the titles for all the different pieces of music in the repertoires of Balinese ensembles, notwithstanding the repetition and con-fusion engendered when, as often happens, the same name is used for two unrelated compositions. Conversely, neighboring villages sometimes use different names for one and the same piece! Equally confusing but far more demanding of scrutiny is the matter of regional variation. Rarely is a single piece of music played precisely the same way by any two groups. It may only be on the level of minute detail, such as a turn in a kotekan rhythm or the ordering of a sequence of angsels, or it may be some more substantial component of the music—but these differences are justly treasured by musicians. "This is how we play it in our village!" is a frequently heard boast. Sadly, these strains of individuality are today under siege. It is often difficult for regional styles to hold their own against the democratizing effects of mass media and centralized education in a fast-shrinking world. Negara and Amlapura, at opposite ends of the island, are no longer as far away from each other as they once were.

Fortunately, the family of ensembles has so far proved mostly impervious to the forces conspiring against stylistic diversity. Kebyar threatened to eclipse some of its ancestors for a time, but the danger seems to have passed. Some ensembles have outlived their functional role in Balinese life, but academics and preserva-tionists are certain to keep them alive for the foreseeable future. In the meantime the whole world of Balinese music is there to be heard by adventurous music lovers. Most of it is readily accessible; hearing certain kinds may take a little advance planning. All of it is well worth the effort. And if the opportunity to hear a live performance cannot be arranged, most everything is available on recordings.

The survey of gamelans undertaken in the following pages is far from exhaus-tive. It covers the most important styles and a few more esoteric ones, providing information about the tuning, instruments, traditional context, and any note-worthy musical idiosyncrasies. There is also mention of which villages host the most prominent representatives of the genre. In this regard it should be noted that the KOKAR/SMKI and STSI conservatories own, between them, at least one set of instruments for every type of gamelan, but these are mainly for study purposes and as such are not classified here along with the indigenous groups. We begin with the bronze ensembles, move on to gamelans in which bamboo is the primary sound-producing material, and introduce some sacred ensembles and miscellany. The chapter concludes with an overview of Balinese vocal music genres.

PART I: BRONZE GAMELAN ENSEMBLES

Gamelan Gong Kebyar

Throughout this book gamelan gong kebyar has been the "default" ensemble for discussing musical instruments and technicalities because it is the orchestra that visitors are most likely to encounter in a formal performance setting, and the kind of gamelan that most Balinese are likely to know something about. There are many who bemoan kebyar's near-hegemony, but such certainly is the reality. If kebyar's resources have indeed proved to be a fertile ground for musical development, perhaps that can be attributed to its birth as a secular and populist ensemble, independent of ritual constraints and the behests of nobility. Gong kebyar has absorbed and processed all of the old styles on which it is directly based, filched a bit of material from ensembles with which it has only a tangential relationship, and above all synthesized all of this to produce a dazzling, ultra-modern repertoire of its own. It is, as ethnologist Miguel Covarrubias wrote, "the modern concert orchestra par excellence".[1]

Kebyar is usually translated as "to burst open," like a flower in sudden bloom, or "to flare up," like a match. The word itself, heavily stressed on the second syllable and with a pronounced roll on the "r," is a perfect onomatopoetic simulation of the ensemble's signature sound: an explosive, throbbing unison attack. The instruments are tuned to a five-tone pelog mode with a moderately fast paired tuning that emphasizes their rich resonance. A full battery of tuned bronze metallophones, an assortment of gongs, cengceng, suling and large kendang all conspire to create a sound of riveting power.

The music of the gamelan gong kebyar exploits the particular capabilities of the instruments in the ensemble. The 10-key range of the 4 pemades, 4 kantilans and the ugal make broad and adventurous melodies possible. The reyong, composed of twelve small gongs, or "pots" and played by four musicians, is used in a number of ways which make a salient contribution to the music. Sometimes it bursts free from the texture to play dazzling "solos" (quartets, actually, since there are four musicians involved) on its own. Another characteristic reyong sound is ocak-ocakan, a combination of 8 pots sounded together in a brassy chord and

---

[1] Covarrubias, Miguel, Island of Bali, Alfred A. Knopf, New York, 1937.

combined with the kendang and cengceng. The pots are also played on the lower rim, which results in a sound similar to that of the cengceng. And of course it also plays along melodically, fitting in with the rest of the ensemble in a more conventional manner.

At the time of its inception, kebyar music was largely a hodgepodge of borrowed material and pastiches clothed in musical modernisms. It began to accumulate its own repertoire after the 1920s, when a dancer from Tabanan village named Maria (Mah-ree-yhe) took the Balinese scene by storm. His creations interpreted the capricious nature of the new music with free form choreographies that featured intricate movements of the upper body and a wide range of facial expressions. The Kebyar Duduk, or sitting kebyar, and Kebyar Trompong, in which the dancer performs upon the trompong amid great histrionics, swept the island, and Maria was instantly in demand everywhere as a teacher of the new style.

Maria's creations helped to coin an entire genre known as *tari lepas*—free dances. Free in this context refers not to the choreography, as most tari lepas music and dance are meticulously planned down to the last angsel, but rather to the brevity of the performance and its independence from any larger theatrical form. Kebyar Duduk, Kebyar Trompong, and dozens of others that subsequently joined the repertoire now form the substance of an evening's kebyar performance, augmented with some more classical dances—Baris, for example, and perhaps even Legong. Other important tari lepas include *Oleg Tambulilingan* (created by Maria in 1951 for the Peliatan gamelan's world tour), which portrays two bumblebees in courtship, and the powerful *Teruna Jaya* (Victorious Youth) from North Bali, a long and difficult dance of great subtlety and beauty that has become a true Balinese classic. Teruna Jaya is a virtuosic effort for both musicians and dancers and is considered to be the quintessential kebyar-style piece. One reliable test of a drummer's mettle is the ease with which he can negotiate a performance of it.

Rounding out tari lepas performances are the new instrumental compositions, the real medium for musical experimentation. From the early days such pieces featured, among other revolutionary musical devices, the occasional abandonment of colotomic principles, the substitution of free rhythm for steady pulse, abrupt stops and starts, and musical forms based around a series of melodic snippets rather than a substantial main movement. Melodies of breadth and scope gave way to a musical language that aimed for virtuosity, speed and special effects. The novelty could not last, of course, but the most gifted musicians were ultimately able to transcend the limits of music based on such superficial notions to create works of great elegance and integrity.

The more or less standard form for kebyar instrumental compositions (*kreasi baru*, as they are usually called) that emerged during the middle of the century consists of five sections separated by transition passages. There are generally two ways to begin a piece. One is the "*kebyar*" proper—a jagged, irregular and forceful melody played in perfect unison by the entire ensemble. Only the kempli is

Gamelan gong kebyar, fronted by the trompong, playing a modernized lelambatan melody.

silent, as no regular beat is intended. The amount of practice needed to perfect the coordination of such unstable rhythms is evident, and the effect in performance is electric. Another kind of opening is the *gineman*—a series of short phrases separated by pauses. Each of the phrases may involve a different combination of instruments, but the predominant sound is that of little bursts of kotekan and melody played by the gangsas, calungs and jegogans. Three internal sections, connected to each other by freely composed links, succeed to the opening. They showcase, in any order, interlocking rhythmic variations for the drums, gangsas, and the reyong. A finale for the whole gamelan closes the piece in a boisterous and flamboyant fashion.

Most kreasi baru have shown themselves to be pretty ephemeral; only some pieces have demonstrated staying power. The reason for this is not necessarily connected to any notions of quality, rather it is a function of the great quantity of compositions that have appeared. Groups tiring of a given piece simply request new ones from their resident director or from an outside composer. A few have become standards in the repertoire, though. *Gambang Suling*, composed in the 1960s and based partly on a popular Javanese melody of the period, is one such piece. *Kapi Raja* and *Jaya Semara* are two nearly identical kebyar-style compositions that have also proven very durable.

The short history of kebyar has already borne witness to the rise and fall of a pantheon of musical giants. In the beginning the Singaraja area monopolized the scene with famous groups in the neighboring villages of Jagaraga and Sawan. The former was the birthplace of the influential drummer and teacher Gede Manik. These villages (and many others in North Bali) still have active gamelan associations, but their island-wide fame has diminished. From the 30s to the 60s the crown was passed between a number of villages around Denpasar—Belaluan, Sadmertha, and Sibang, to name a few—and the village of Peliatan some 20-odd kilometers to the north. Pressure to innovate was fierce in those days, and intergroup competition was cutthroat. Tales of spies sent to observe rival groups' rehearsals and enormous fees paid to secure exclusive rights to a teacher for a new piece (plans often frustrated by sabotage and shady dealing) illustrate the ruthless zeal with which the new music was propagated.

Two groups that emerged in the 1960s are still very famous today, although they are more or less dormant unless fulfilling obligations to perform sacred music in the temple or playing for some other special occasion. These are in the villages of Geladag, south of Denpasar, and Pindha, near Blahbatuh in Gianyar district. Each is situated in an area that has been musically fertile since long before the advent of kebyar. Mention of either group will kindle flames of near-nationalistic fervor in the eyes of Balinese who live anywhere around either of those places. Both maintain expansive repertoires of lelambatan for use in the temple as well as an array of modern dance and music pieces, which in many cases were given their first and definitive performances by these groups. To hear the best of kebyar while in Bali, it is well worth inquiring as to whether or not either the Pindha or Geladag group is engaged for a temple or recreational performance. If not, it is not difficult to commission something, even on short notice (details on how to do this will be given in the last chapter). These are phenomenally proficient orchestras, among the tightest and and most polished musical organizations in the world. Hearing them on their home turf can be one of the best reasons to get off the beaten track in Bali.

No gamelan in the past quarter century or so (save for the conservatory groups) has achieved enough fame to challenge the supremacy of Pindha and Geladag. One close contender emerged in the 1970s in the village of Perean, Tabanan district. A recording of their ensemble from that period displays the absolute summit of gamelan speed and virtuosity: kotekan played at a rate of 200 beats per minute. At four subdivisions per beat that breaks down to 800 notes per minute, or an average of 400 notes each for polos and sangsih parts, which in turn translates to almost 7 notes per player per second! Can one conceive of 25 people doing *anything* together that fast? All of this was executed with crystalline clarity and accompanied, one might surmise, by facial expressions of utter nonchalance and boredom during performance. Regrettably, Perean's group disbanded soon after those recordings were made. Some of the musicians and their families subsequently transmigrated to Sumatra on an Indonesian government resettlement and land development program. In the spring of 1989, however, a revival organized by some of those who remained behind led to some very strong comeback performances.

Today the kebyar scene is dominated by music made at the conservatories, and by the groups that participate in the yearly Festival Gong. For the latter, each spring two different groups—one male and one female—from each of Bali's 8 districts are chosen to represent their area with a number of standard and newly created works. The rotation ensures that over a period of years as many villages as possible participate and, for better or worse, keeps the public eye from focusing on any particular one for too long. The competing groups are judged each June by an island-wide panel of experts and winners are chosen.

Mention should be made of some prominent individuals active currently. By far the single most revered older musician in all of Balinese music today is I Wayan Beratha, whose father Made Regog was the head of the gamelan from Belaluan in the 1930s. Beratha's influence as a drummer and composer is felt everywhere. He is also active as a tuner and gamelan merchant. Other important senior figures are I Nyoman Rembang of Sesetan, Badung (also a scholar and prominent music historian), I Wayan Begeg of Pangkung, Tabanan, I Putu Sumiasa of Kedis, Buleleng, and I Wayan Tembres of Blangsinga, Gianyar, who will be profiled in Chapter 8. One of the most outstanding young performers is I Wayan Suweca of Denpasar, whose prowess as a drummer is well-known. Suweca is a lecturer at the conservatory, and his colleagues both in and out of school comprise the finest talents of his generation. There are too many to note here individually, but there are enough of them to guarantee the vitality of gamelan gong kebyar for some time to come.

Gamelan Semar Pegulingan / Gamelan Pelegongan

For Balinese these two closely related ensembles evoke pleasant and ethereal images of a not-too-distant past whose elegant sensibilities have lately been trampled by too much modernism too fast. It is certainly true that there are only a handful of these high-pitched, sweet-sounding gamelans extant now, whereas there were hundreds only 50 years ago. Semar Pegulingan is a seven-tone pelog ensemble with a repertoire derived from the gamelan gambuh. It features a trompong on the lead melody part. The ornamentation instruments are of but 7 keys each (one octave range), as are the jegogans and calungs. No reyong is present. The large gong is supplanted by the kempur and the kempli by the boss-less kajar. The kendang are small too, and there are a variety of tiny, chiming cymbal-like instruments that fill out the orchestra. The music of Semar Pegulin-gan is sensuous and perfumed, with all manner of plaintive melodies resulting from the added dimensions of the full 7-tone scale.

There are only a few surviving 7-tone Semar Pegulingan groups in Bali with long histories. One is in the village of Kamasan, Klungkung district, and the others are in Denpasar at Banjars Pagan Kelod, Sesetan Kaja, and Tampak Gangsul. The latter will likely soon be defunct as the younger generation has not learned the tradition, which is currently carried only by some very old men. In Kamasan the music has been nourished and the ensemble is active, at least at

Gamelan Pelegongan in Teges Kanginan.

ceremony time. Young people in the village have taken a special interest in the music of late as well. Luckily, the conservatories have been instrumental in promoting awareness of Semar Pegulingan music, and as a result there are signs of a revival in a few places. Banjar Abiankapas in Denpasar recently acquired an ensemble, and musicians in Ubud are experimenting with a brand new set of instruments that can be used for both Semar Pegulingan and kebyar repertoires.

The same combination of instruments mentioned above, but restricted to the 5-tone pelog-Selisir mode, and augmented by two genders, are also referred to as Semar Pegulingan. The genders are of 13, 14 or 15 keys each and are played in octaves with two mallets, which produces a delicate sound that adds a lilting, wistful air to the music. In some compositions, when the trompong is not used, this kind of gamelan is also called *pelegongan* because that particular configuration of instruments is primarily associated with performances of the classical *legong keraton* dances. This is the gamelan that reigned during the colonial period and charmed Colin McPhee into devoting himself so assiduously to Balinese music. Pelegongan music is by turns majestic and moving, playful and winsome, and without any of the aggressive tendencies of kebyar. For gamelan connoisseurs, it is the classiest and wittiest music on the island.

Legong keraton (or simply legong) is not a single dance, as it is often misunderstood to be, but in fact a whole genre of choreographies, each with its own musical accompaniment. The *Lasem* story is the most popular. It portrays an old Javanese tale of the kidnapping of a princess and her abductor's confrontation by

7-tone Semar Pegulingan at Banjar Pagan Kelod, Denpasar.

a bird of ill omen while on the way to do battle for his honor. Also an important part of the pelegongan repertoire is the *Calonarang* play, a 16th century tale of witchcraft and terror in a Balinese village which features the beloved dragon-protector Barong and the despised witch Rangda. The Calonarang music for the *sisya*, or dance of the witch's disciples, is one of the most haunting and beautiful melodies in all of Balinese music. No pelegongan performance would be complete without an instrumental piece or two. Some of these are adapted from the 7-tone Semar Pegulingan repertoire; others were bequeathed by the patriarch of pelegongan music, I Lotring, or by one of the many other composers active during his era.

There are wonderful pelegongan/Semar Pegulingan ensembles to be heard in the villages of Tista, near Kerambitan, Binoh, northwest of Denpasar, Teges Kanginan, just east of Peliatan, and Ketewel, near Sukawati. The legong tradition in Ketewel is notable for its close connections to the history of the form. The village possesses a unique set of eight extremely sacred female masks that are used in performances of a progenitor of the modern legong, the *legong bidedari*. This dance is said to have originated in the visions of a priest who lived in Ketewel near the end of the 19th century. Bidedari are angels; the priest reported witnessing a beautiful dance by two angels in heaven while meditating. Choreographies were later devised, on the instructions of the priest, to reproduce what he had seen. The young dancers were required to perform with the masks so that the spirits of the angels might enter them. Later, in the early part of this century, the king of nearby Sukawati village oversaw the adaptation and transformation of the legong bidedari choreographies into what evolved as the modern legong. The sacred masks, however, are still danced at important ceremonies in Ketewel.

In Peliatan village the excellent Tirtha Sari group gives a weekly performance with some elegant and authentic pieces, as well as others that have been thoroughly kebyar-ized. Important personages in the pelegongan world include I Wayan Sinti and his father I Ketut Sadia of Binoh (Sinti teaches at the KOKAR/SMKI conservatory). Three recently deceased elder statesmen—I Made Grindem of the Teges group, Anak Agung Gde Raka of Saba village, and I Made Lebah of Peliatan—were particularly celebrated and revered. Lebah's career stretched back to 1931, when he performed with the group from Peliatan in Paris and romanced both the Parisian public and the group's legong dancers—one of whom he later married—with his agile drumming. Throughout the 30s Lebah was Colin McPhee's guide, chauffeur, teacher, and all around right-hand man. Up to his death in late 1996 he continued to teach gamelan from time to time.

Gamelan Gender Wayang

Many visitors to Bali hear their first Balinese music played on a pair or quartet of gender wayang, placed off to the side in the hotel lobby. Being relegated to background accompaniment is too often the status quo for this elite chamber gamelan. But its players, over the generations, have slyly exacted their revenge by concocting the most complex, technically difficult, and respected music in all of Bali.

Four ten-key, slendro-tuned genders make up the complete ensemble, although in some specialized contexts drums and gongs are added. Two of the genders are tuned in a medium register and two an octave higher. It is perfectly acceptable for only the larger pair to be used, however, since all of the musical parts are present with two players. Each musician uses two mallets to play independent left and right hand parts. Generally the players' right hands play kotekan while the left hands support this with melody, but there are all sorts of exceptions to this. Gender wayang music can feature two different, simultaneous kotekans, or even a low-register kotekan underpinning a high, slow-moving melody. The variety of textures and nuances cultivated in the performance of the music is tremendous.

Gender is most often heard at *wayang kulit* (shadow play) performances, but it is also traditionally used to provide instrumental music for tooth filing ceremonies and, strangely enough, at cremations, where its tones are usually lost in the roar of the crowd. But the ensemble's natural environment is behind the flickering images of the Hindu *Mahabharata* epic stories played out on the shadow play screen, matching every detail of the puppeteer's performance with an elaborate musical response.

Shadow plays are preceded by one or more of the many dazzling free instrumental compositions from the ensemble's repertoire. Famous ones include *Sekar Gendot*, *Sekar Sungsiang*, and *Merak Ngelo*. Then a long overture, the *Pemungkah*,

Dalang Nartha with gender wayang musicians from Sukawati. I Wayan Loceng is at Nartha's rear-left.

accompanies the *dalang*, or puppeteer, as he carefully removes all of the puppets from the wooden box in which they are kept, exposes them to the world of the screen, and then replaces all but the ones to be used for that performance. Next he introduces the *kayonan*, or tree-of-life puppet, intones a series of evocative verses, and the play begins. For the duration of the performance the gender players provide music for all of the dalang's songs, for love scenes and scenes of enchantment or despair, for changes of story locale, and for the plentiful battles that always make up the play's climactic moments.

Balinese musicians who do not play gender wayang are usually in awe of their counterparts who do, such is the reputation of the music's difficulty. The gender players themselves, proud to have mastered such a challenging art form, are more often than not fanatically dedicated to it. When two such musicians from different regions meet, especially if there is a set of gender around, there is bound to be much animated discussion about stylistic differences and the details of performing particular pieces. Regional variation in gender wayang compositions is the most drastic of all Balinese gamelans, perhaps because the intimate size of the ensemble has always made it feasible for individual musicians to assert themselves and make changes in the inherited repertoire that have distinct and personalized characteristics.

The inseparable arts of puppetry and gender wayang have a long history of cultivation in Sukawati village. Today the reigning gender king of Sukawati is I Wayan Loceng. A brilliant and dedicated teacher, Loceng is conversant in all aspects of puppetry, including the mythology and linguistics behind it, as well as being a master of the music. I Wayan Wija, a young and extremely popular dalang from Sukawati, has developed the *wayang tantri*, using stories from the Tantri series. These tales are roughly analogous to "Aesop's Fables", with their sylvan setting and animal characters. For this he has devised an entirely original set of puppets and a new instrumental combination which uses pelog-tuned genders playing in gender wayang style, drums, and gongs. Wija's latest project is a set of dinosaur puppets, to be used in a shadow play set in prehistoric times.

Other proponents of gender wayang are no less gifted or influential. Musician, dancer, and puppeteer I Nyoman Sumandhi of the KOKAR/SMKI conservatory is originally from Tunjuk village in Tabanan, where his father Rajeg still enjoys an active career in the arts that he passed to his son. In Denpasar I Wayan Konolan and many of his children are much in demand as performers of this style. There are gender wayang styles in North Bali at, among other places, Munduk and Tejakula, in Karangasem at Padangkertha, at Teges village near Peliatan, and in private homes around Bali where the music is studied for the satisfying challenge it provides.

Gamelan Angklung

At temple festivals, the exuberance of the 4-tone gamelan angklung's melodies ring out in bold contrast to the solemn and grave lelambatan compositions often heard playing simultaneously right across the courtyard. While to many outsiders the slendro-derived tuning of the gamelan produces a mood of playfulness and charm, to the Balinese it is sentimental, bittersweet, and an indispensable component of the atmosphere at any meaningful ceremony.

A modern Balinese gamelan angklung comprises 8–12 4-keyed metallophones used for melody or kotekan, a reyong of 8 pots, 2 jegogans, a small kempur, 2 tiny drums, cengceng, suling and a kind of kempli called *tawa-tawa*. The word *angklung* originally referred to a bamboo rattle which produces but one tone when shaken. Ensembles of these, tuned to a scale and shaken in alternation to create melodies, are still common in West Java. In Bali they used to be played in conjunction with the bronze instruments,[2] but today they are rarely seen, although people often lament their demise nostalgically.

There is a large repertoire of compositions for gamelan angklung. It is full of whimsical short pieces with names like *Goak Maling Taloh* (Crow Steals Eggs) and *Katak Nongkek* (Croaking Frog) and longer pieces of considerable breadth. Having only 4 keys per instrument would seem a limitation, and certainly no one would claim that gamelan angklung has as great an expressive range as any of the larger bronze ensembles. Yet as a rule angklung music is full of supple melodies and inventive kotekans, which often breathe and flow in quite unexpected directions. A number of angklungs around the island, particularly in the north, use

---

[2] Colin McPhee reintroduced them in Sayan village in 1938, when he bought a Gamelan Angklung for the village children. (See the passage at the beginning of Chapter One.)

4-keyed gangsas in the gamelan angklung, Mas.   *Jegogans carry the melody in gamelan angklung.*

the full 5-tone slendro scale for the additional possibilities it provides, with the size of the instruments expanded accordingly, sometimes up to as many as seven keys. This serves to drastically reduce the constraints imposed by the 4-tone version, substantially altering the personality of the resultant music in the process.

There may be more sets of gamelan angklung in Bali than there are gamelan gong kebyar. Most villages have at least one or two. The village of Mas alone had, at last count, seven; their players have a tough time with scheduling, because a local temple festival lasts only a few days! But the temple is not the only place to hear angklung. Because of the instruments' portability, they are often strung up on bamboo poles and carried in processions. Some tari lepas and kreasi baru have been adapted for the ensemble, thus creating the secular sub-genre of *angklung kebyar*. Ketut Partha, a teacher at the STSI conservatory, is well known for his contributions to the development of this style. One of the most famous traditional angklung gamelans can be found in the village of Sidan, on the road between Gianyar and Bangli.

Gamelan Gong Gde / Gamelan Gong

The enormous *gong gde* (great gong) ensemble, ancestral progenitor of gong kebyar and indispensable arm of Bali's bygone royal courts, is a splendid anachronism today. Every facet of gong gde music—the slow, regal tempi, the bald simplicity of the melodic style, the crushing weight of the bronze keys and the mallets used to strike them—exudes majesty, pomp and ceremony mighty

Giant sarons (or gangsa jongkok) in the gamelan gong gde.

enough to call the Gods to attention.

More is better in gong gde. Extra calungs and jegogans, two trompongs, gigantic drums and gongs, and pair after pair of large cengceng and saron-style gangsas make up the ensemble, which takes up to 50 people to play. Only the reyong is small, with but four pots. The tunings are dramatic and deep, employing a 5-tone pelog. The gong gde's repertoire of lelambatan and dance music is vast—although one can only imagine how many more pieces there were at one time, when this orchestra's presence was requisite in the courts.

Up until the establishment of the colonial administration and the dismantling of the feudal system in Bali, the gamelan gong gde was one of the foremost symbols of the courts' opulence. No village could have ever afforded to maintain an orchestra of that size. But by the late 19th century many villages were casting scaled-down versions of the gong gde that could approximate the sound of the original without unduly straining municipal and temple budgets. This ensemble, rarely heard today, became known simply as the gamelan gong.

History has shown that the gamelan gong served some important functions at the time. It helped to disseminate the music of the royal court in the villages, and it also exposed that music to the influence of other gamelan styles. In gamelan gong music, for instance, lelambatan melodies were ornamented with simple kotekans on the gangsas for the first time, whereas in gong gde ornament is limited to the tiny reyong used. Gamelan gong served as a kind of transitional phase before the advent of gamelan gong kebyar, which quickly proved up to subsuming all of its functions. By the time of Indonesian independence most gamelan gong had been melted down and recast as the streamlined kebyars. There are some left; one is in Demulih village, near Bangli.

With the exception of an ensemble that is kept in Denpasar, the few gong gde still played in Bali are scattered around Bangli district. There is one in the village of Sulahaan which is reputed to have been bequeathed by the king of Bangli when the court disbanded. Another is kept in the temple overlooking Lake Batur, where it plays regularly for festivals. The powerful tolling of the gong gde during a moonlit ceremony is a stirring musical reminder of a Bali that is now part of the past.

PART II: BAMBOO GAMELAN ENSEMBLES

Tingklik and Gamelan Joged Bumbung

The Balinese gamelans that use bamboo tubes or slats rather than bronze slabs for keys are the true folk music of Bali, in the sense that they were never courtly arts. This in no way implies, however, that the music made on them is in any way simpler or less rigorous in construction. It is only that the occasions on which they are played are more often impromptu and meant mostly to be for fun and diversion. Bamboo music is very much on an earthly plane, refreshingly free of any pretenses to sublimity.

Tingklik is the most common name for a bamboo instrument made of a series of tubes tuned to a scale and strung up in ascending order in a simple frame. Most any Balinese with a little acquired expertise could easily construct one by just using materials found growing in his or her backyard; doubtless the origin of the tingklik traces to some leisurely tinkerers and their serendipitous experimentations in at-home bamboo laboratories. Long before anyone had the idea of combining groups of such instruments into ensembles, people were improvising melodies on them in their spare time. From these modest beginnings, a world of music grew.

Most tingklik are tuned to a slendro scale and played with two spindly, rubber-tipped mallets. Bamboo has virtually no sustaining resonance on its own and emits a very dry sound when struck, so the tubes need not be damped between tones like bronze keys. This makes tingklik easier to play than gender, but coordination between left and right hands is still a problem. Pairs of tingkliks play melody and kotekan in a kind of gender wayang style when heard, as they often are, in hotels and restaurants. The sweet and unobtrusive charm of their music, often augmented with a melodious suling or two, has a great appeal for many visitors to Bali.

A group of four or more tingkliks with added flutes, drums and an ersatz gong made by hanging an enormous bamboo key (metal is sometimes used) over a resonator is called *gamelan joged bumbung*, or just *gamelan joged* for short. It is

Tingklik in gamelan joged bumbung, Singapadu village.

primarily used as an accompaniment for the *joged* dance, wherein a single girl dancer taunts male members of the audience into joining her in a flirtatious and often hilarious improvised duet. The men are not necessarily trained dancers, but they are expected to sink or swim. This creates a little embarrassment sometimes, but more often than not just gales and gales of good-natured laughter.

The origins of *gamelan joged* melodies are usually a mystery, even to the musicians who play them. Some come from popular songs; others have been composed by the players themselves. For tingklik duets and quartets some pieces have been appropriated directly from gamelan gender wayang. Most have anonymous origins, having emerged somewhere along the path of the music's development.

Locating good joged ensembles is difficult, as they seem to form and disband as quickly as their instruments can be constructed or disassembled. There are famous ones near the city of Gianyar and in Sanur that are often in demand to provide an evening's entertainment. Joged groups are frequently engaged by families undertaking a private ceremony that wish to repay the members of their village for the substantial amount of community labor that is always donated on such occasions.

In northern and western Bali, they take their gamelan joged very seriously. In fact western Bali is the only part of the island that perhaps cares a bit more for bamboo music than it does for bronze. Expanded ensembles made from larger and more richly sonorous bamboo play music for joged dancers, pieces transplanted from the kebyar repertoire, and indigenous instrumental works with phenomenal brilliance and clarity. This style of joged is best heard in Jembrana at Tegalcang-kering, in Tabanan at Luwus, and in Buleleng at Sangsit.

Gamelan Jegog

Bamboo grown in west Bali reaches monstrous proportions the likes of which are not known elsewhere on the island. This quirk of nature has been exploited by local musicians with the creation of the *gamelan jegog*, so named for the remarkable *jegogan* that is the sonic core of the ensemble. Individual tubes on these may stretch to an incredible 3 meters in length, with circumferences of 60–65 centimeters.[3] They are so unwieldy that a pair of musicians must sit on top of the frame of the instrument in order to play it. It requires quite a pounding with thick rubber beaters to coax music out of them, but what finally emerges is a sound so powerful that it seems to enter the body through the stomach rather than the ears.

Jegog is tuned to an unusual and haunting 4-tone scale which, it is speculated, was derived from tones 2, 3, 5, and 7 of the full 7-tone pelog (see Chapter Three). All of the instruments have 8 tubes. On the jegogan and the two calungs tuned an octave above them, the 4 right-hand tubes duplicate the tones of those

---

[3] This seems particularly surreal when one recalls that botanically speaking, bamboo is actually just a species of grass.

A festive gamelan jegog ensemble from Tegalcangkering village in West Bali.

on the left, enabling the players to play rolling melodies by alternating left and right hand strokes between notes of the same pitch. The upper register instruments play melodies and kotekans, including a special style of kotekan called *slanketan*, in which individual players negotiate both polos and sangsih at once. Melodic and rhythmic cycles are arranged into episodic compositions, the lengths of which can be prolonged or foreshortened simply by repeating any of the sections more or fewer times.

Great crowds gather when two, three or more *jegog* groups assemble in an open field of an evening to *mabarung*—play competition style. At first, the idea is to scrutinize the quality of the instruments' sound, the musical content and the technical skill of the players. The opening strains of each gamelan's music are carefully examined for these qualities. As the evening progresses, the groups begin to play simultaneously in a cacophony of short, driving ostinato patterns. The focus then shifts to determining who can play louder, harder and for as long as possible without stopping or losing their place in the melody. Shirts soak through with sweat and fingers get ravaged by blisters as musicians push themselves to the absolute limits of their physical abilities in pursuit of such distinctions. Around 2 a.m., after a trial by a jury of peers, the exhausted players finally disperse.

Jegog is extremely popular in Jembrana and getting more so all the time. Any single village may have 5 or 6 active groups. The villages of Tegalcangkering and Sangkaragung are among the best known. A walk down the main street of either of these towns at night is bound to lead to a lively rehearsal hall or two that is filled with the colorfully painted jegog instruments and a group of musicians playing them with abandon. It is worth a trip to this little-visited part of Bali just to hear their ecstatic music.

Gamelan Gandrung

The gandrung ensemble, once popular as an accompaniment to a joged-like dance of the same name, bears mention even though it is nearly extinct. The 5-tone pelog-tuned instruments are constructed of wooden slats suspended over bamboo resonators much in the manner of genders, and are played in octaves with a mallet in each hand. The ensemble also includes the usual complement of kendang and other percussion. The gandrung style of playing kotekan is famous among Balinese musicians for being second in complexity only to that of gender wayang. Even though the music is rarely heard today, its influence is felt in many kebyar pieces.

During the colonial period gandrung ensembles proliferated. Today the only extant gandrung groups are in Ketapian Kelod, on the outskirts of Denpasar, and in Tegunungan, south of Kemenuh village in Gianyar district. The former achieved some renown during the 1920s, when it was led by Nyoman Kaler, a famous drummer, composer and choreographer. But Kaler's services were much in demand and he did not stay with the group long. In subsequent years the flirtatious gandrung dance, too, fell from esteem in the public's eye. Recently, Ketapian's village elders were wise enough to declare the ensemble *keramat*—sacred—thereby ensuring its survival through mandatory usage in temple rituals.

PART III: SACRED AND RARE ENSEMBLES

Gamelan Selonding

Gamelan selonding is one of a group of 7-tone pelog ensembles in Bali distinguished by their ancient origins and extremely sacred connotations. They are probably the oldest ensembles on the island, predating the gamelan gambuh. Selonding is associated with the Bali Aga, or so-called pre-Hindu villages scattered about the hills of eastern Bali. Many of the instruments used, and most all of the compositions played on it are considered to have been bequeathed to the villagers by deities in the mythological past.

These gamelans are used only in specific ritual contexts, and elaborate offerings must be made prior to playing them. The instruments themselves, as well as the compositions played on them, are indispensable components in the successful completion of annual ceremonial rites; by extension they are also considered necessary for maintaining the general spiritual well-being of the village and its members.

Selonding is the only gamelan with keys cast from iron. The keys are strung

Iron-keyed gamelan selonding (Bugbug village).

up over low troughs and played with club-shaped mallets in an unusual two-handed technique. Although the makeup of the gamelan varies from village to village, it is often composed exclusively of these instruments, although a set of cengceng may be added for music that accompanies dance. Selonding melody and figuration has a soft rippling sound quite distinct from the piercing sonority of bronze.

Some well-known selonding ensembles are kept in the eastern villages of Asak, Bungaya, and Tangkas. The village of Tenganan is notable for its 3 selonding ensembles, which are stored in individual sheds lined up north-south along the terraced main street. These are acknowledged to be man-made copies of an original, God-given gamelan, which is never actually used in performance. The ones that may be played are brought out at festival time and set up on raised platforms within sight and reach only of the specially designated performers. The instruments must undergo costly purification rites if their sanctity is degraded by the touch or glance of outsiders.

This last statement requires qualification. After centuries of fiercely guarding selonding's purity Tenganan has, in the past decade or so, relaxed some restrictions. The village instruments are still protected, but recordings have been made and distributed commercially—a heretofore unthinkable blasphemy! Copies of the ensembles are now in the possession of the conservatories, where students and faculty learn the ancient music in a purely secular environment. Nyoman Windha, a gifted young composer, has created a major new work for Selonding

The famous gamelan gambang from Asak village performs at a variety of ritual occasions.

instruments called *Bali Aga*. These developments have aroused the protests of some observers, but the liberties taken were granted by the Tenganese themselves, so it would seem that the case must rest there.

Gamelan Gambang

The brittle and austere sound of the 7-tone *gamelan gambang* has long been important at cremations, at temple festivals in East Bali, and at other selected ceremonies. It is allied in function with the gamelan selonding where both are found in the same village, but the gambang's domain is more geographically diverse; it is found in northern and southern Bali as well. That the 4 wooden gambang xylophones used in the ensemble have close relatives of the same name in Javanese gamelan is an indication of the instrument's long, venerable history.

In Bali each gambang is played with a pair of Y-shaped mallets, the twin tips of which are spaced so as to strike tones an octave apart. With the 4 players' 8 hands in constant motion, a dense and involuted kotekan is generated. As in the gamelan gambuh and other 7-tone ensembles, only five of the seven notes are used in any single composition. In gamelan gambang music, virtually all possible distillations of five-note modes from the original seven are found in the repertoire. For the gamelan gambang at Bebetin village, near Singaraja, the modes are named according to the best-known piece in which they are used. The five-note group used in the important composition *Semarandhana*, for example, is called "Semarandhana mode" even when it is used in other pieces. Of course, as with

A cak in Teges, created by the Javanese choreographer Sardono.

all systems of nomenclature in Bali, there is considerable variance from one village to the next.

Completing the gamelan are a pair of 7-key bronze saron-style metallo-phones that ring out brightly with the core melody. This melody is nearly always stated in the characteristic rhythm of 5 + 3 counts, an uneven division of an ordinary 8-beat phrase that is instantly identifiable to most Balinese musicians as "gambangan rhythm." It is often used in gamelan pelegongan and kebyar compositions for the distinctive flavor that it adds.

Gambang compositions, because of their continuous staid rhythm, are very difficult to learn. None of the four gambangs' keys are laid out in the same way, and each of the four players' parts is different from the others. Moreover, individual pieces are closely connected to verse forms in classical poetry, and it is said to be a frustrating experience at best to attempt to play the music without having mastered the poems first. Perhaps for this reason gambang is usually attractive to scholarly and literary-minded individuals. Well known gambang traditions are extant in many villages, among them Sempidi, near Denpasar, and Asak, Karangasem district.

Gamelan Luang/Gamelan Gong Bheri

Two other rare and sacred ensembles merit passing mention. *Gamelan luang*, now found only in Sukawati and Singapadu, Gianyar; Kerambitan, Tabanan; Tangkas, Klungkung, and a few other places, is an archaic, 7-tone relative of the gamelan gong gde that combines a mixture of bronze and bamboo instruments. The instrumentation of each luang is unique. The repertoire of compositions is large, containing many compositions that equal lelambatan in their scope and grandeur. In some villages there are close connections to the gamelan gambang tradition as well. The Kerambitan group, following the lead of the selondings from Tenganan village, has recorded and issued a cassette of "New Compositions for Gamelan Luang."

Renon, a village near Sanur that has recently become the seat of Bali's central government, is the only village that cultivates an unusual ensemble of gongs, drums and cengceng called *gamelan gong bheri*, which is used to accompany an even more unusual dance, the *Baris Cina* (Chinese Baris). The dance has nothing to do with the country, but the instruments of the gamelan are said to have come centuries ago from a Chinese trading ship that ran aground off the coast nearby. The bossless gongs in the gamelan do in fact resemble Chinese tam-tams, so there may well be some truth to the story.

PART IV: OTHER BALINESE ENSEMBLES

Gamelan Bebonangan/Beleganjur

The 4, 5 or 6-part interlocking rhythms of the giant cengceng kopyak, as used in the gamelan gong gde, form the basis for certain genres of Balinese music that thrive on the intensity that those patterns generate. One such ensemble is the *bebonangan* or, as it is popularly called, *beleganjur*, a fixture in virtually all religious processions. It is next to impossible to drive around Bali of an afternoon without encountering at least one of these boisterous marching bands bringing up the rear in a parade of colorfully dressed Balinese.

Gamelan bebonangan is actually just a gong kebyar without metallophones, plus several sets of the cengceng. The gongs are strung up on bamboo poles to facilitate carrying them, and the drummers, playing with mallets, hang their instruments around their necks with a cord. To carry the reyong, some of the pots are removed from their frame and distributed, one to a player. Polos and sangsih are thus further subdivided into two parts each, which results in a 4-part kotekan. Such an arrangement makes the music especially difficult to coordinate, particularly while walking.

The word *bebonangan* comes from *bonang*, the Javanese word for the type of small gongs used on the reyong and trompong. *Beleganjur* means, roughly, 'walking army' in Old Javanese, thus signifying marching music. Driven by an authoritative gilak pattern provided by the gongs and kempli, the cengcengs, reyong and kendang engage in a three-way musical dialogue of commanding power. The instrumental groups fade in and out of the texture, meeting occasionally for a series of angsel patterns, only to diverge again, melting into the hypnotic pulsing of the gongs. A more compelling type of marching music has yet to be devised.

Beleganjur is loud, infectious, exciting to play, and a particular favorite with young people in Bali today. Ketut Gde Asnawa, a composer from Kaliungu Kaja, Denpasar, started a craze in 1986 when he formed a recreational beleganjur group in his banjar. He extended the traditional patterns by elaborating the angsel sequences and introducing more kotekan and drum variations. In the few years since then, beleganjur groups have appeared everywhere. This has led to popular competitions in which twenty or more groups assemble and file in parade fashion past seated jurors, who evaluate the contestants on their ensemble skill and even on the theatricality of their presentation, which has become a big part of the fun. Make up, outrageous costumes, and even little choreographed stepping routines are routinely tossed into the act, adding a tongue-in-cheek dimension to the festivities.

Cak (Kecak)

Cak (often called *kecak* and also known as the "Monkey Chant") is a theatrical performance that enacts the rescue of princess Sita from the demon-king Rawana by an army of monkeys, an important episode in the Hindu *Ramayana* epic. For cak, no instrument is used but the human voice. The lead dancers and actors are encircled by a male chorus that portrays the monkeys in sound and movement. There are singing parts distributed amongst the chorus and dancers, but the main purpose of the chorus is to emulate the hordes of attackers with a cloud of percussive vocal effects. The syllable "cak!" ("cha'!"), spat out repetitively by the 100 monkeys through clenched teeth in a set of staccato interlocking rhythms creates a sound that evokes the frightening turbulence of the scene.

The cak rhythms are similar to cengceng kopyak patterns. There are up to seven independent parts, none any more than 4 beats in duration. One strong-lunged member of the chorus is called upon to chant a continuous simulated kempli beat (the syllable 'pung' sung in a high-pitched and nasal tone is used) with which the interlocking monkeys align themselves. Dancers playing the part of Rawana or the monkey general Hanuman prance about, exhorting or taunting the army to intensify or restrain their chanting with guttural sounds ranging from bursts of controlled rage to uninhibited whoops. At times the chorus breaks from its 'cak' patterns to interject with demonic hisses and yells, or, depending on the dramatic situation, subdued and pious singing.

Cak is and always has been a tourist performance. Walter Spies, the renowned artist and Baliphile, commissioned its creation while he was living in Bali during the 30s. The idea for the chorus was inspired by certain trance dances in which a similar type of group male singing has an exorcistic role. Cak is still performed often, notably in the village of Bona, near Gianyar, where it was first done, and also at the Denpasar Art Center. I Wayan Dibia, an important contemporary choreographer, took an interest in cak during the early 1980s and devised several ingenious new versions of it, one of which was designed to be enacted on Kuta beach at sunset. Tourists and villagers alike stared in fascination as the dancers, freed from the confines of the normal performance arena, splashed through the water, the cak rhythms blending seamlessly into the roar of the surf.

Gamelan Miscellany

Our list of Balinese ensembles could easily be extended far beyond this point, but a few additional lines will be made to suffice for the present. There is *tektekan*, a form of beleganjur in which the cengceng are replaced or augmented by bamboo sticks or wooden cowbells. Another "giant" gamelan of West Bali (cousin of the bamboo *gamelan jegog*) is the *kendang mabarung*, which features gargantuan drums carved in a single piece out of an entire tree trunk. The *gamelan batel*, a set of gender wayang instruments augmented with drums, cymbals and gongs, accompanies certain theatrical forms with stories drawn from the *Ramayana* epic. These include the *wayang wong* masked dance drama and some wayang kulit. *Cakepung*, a spontaneous and rowdy chorus in which voices imitate the different instruments of the gamelan, is popular in the northern and eastern parts of the island. Occasionally one encounters a *gong suling* ensemble, in which half a dozen or so suling of different sizes team up with gongs, cengceng and drums. And the *genggong*, a kind of jew's harp, performs in ensemble as accompaniment to a fairy-tale like dance about a frog-prince.

Balinese Vocal Genres

Unless accompanying a theatrical performance where actors speak and sing, most Balinese gamelan music is instrumental. But there is another world of musical activity closely connected to literature and scripture, where the teaching of morality, philosophy and music are intimately connected. This branch of Balinese music may find its audience in small and private gatherings, or in the inner spiritual world of a high priest in prayer, but is no less significant for not being intended to reach the general public.

The main function of singing in Bali—whether by a soloist or a chorus—is to give voice to classical poetic texts. Save for a few kinds of ancient ritual songs, poetry is written and preserved on *lontar*, leaves of the borassus palm (*borassus flabellifer*). Successive generations of Balinese scribes have continually recopied the works, introducing edits and changes commensurate with their historical or literary perspectives; few new poems in the classical forms are introduced today. The importance of vocal music lies as much with the literary meaning, linguistic conventions and performance context of the poems as it does with their melodic style and voice qualities of the singers. They are conceived of as literature to be "voiced", rather than as a separate aesthetic category of song, though musical detail receives more emphasis in some genres. In performance (a word perhaps only partially appropriate) the totality of features—language, content, timbre and intonation, and setting—are to be considered together.

Sloka are Sanskrit chants employed by *pedanda* (Brahman priests) during rituals and by puppeteers in the wayang kulit as invocations or to convene supernatural forces. A deep, chest-centered, guttural voice quality is used, intended to reverberate through and beyond the body. This is the only current usage of Sanskrit in Bali, and as such evokes the distant, quasi-mythological past of Hindu India. Sloka emphasize inherently charged syllables (such as Ong or Aum) that function as aural metaphors for cosmic unity. Rhythm is free, and melodies are syllabic, static and flat, constrained to at most three tones. Today few Balinese understand Sanskrit, but all can grasp that sloka are a channel linking the present to a sacred realm that transcends history, where mythic time converges with the supernatural forces sustaining the universe. Sloka was probably introduced to Bali during the first stages of Hindu influence, between the sixth and ninth centuries.

Kekawin are lengthy poems composed in Bali and Java beginning in the ninth century. They are written in the Old Javanese language *Kawi*, which is still widely known in Bali but rarely used or studied in Java. Kakawin poetic meters, based faithfully on Indian ones, are called *wirama* or known by the Javanese term *sekar ageng* (sekar here means meter; ageng is large or great). There are over 200 different types, each comprised of three or four line stanzas using a prescribed succession of long and short vowel sounds. There may be as many as 26 syllables in a line, and hundreds of stanzas in a complete text. Voice quality is commandingly deep and resonant.

Performance of *kakawin* is an intrinsically literary event, as they are usually vocalized in small gatherings of popular literary clubs called sekaha *pepaosan* (from *paos*, to read), where they are formally "performed", translated into vernacular Balinese, and interpreted for discussion. Kakawin literature, essentially extinct on Java, thrives in Bali through the sekaha pepaosan and represents an important link to the distant past for ordinary Balinese. Unlike the overtly philosophical and liturgical sloka, *kakawin* conjures up images of the deeds and beliefs of gods and ancestors, and thus has direct relevance for the teaching of morality in contemporary life.

Kidung, written in later forms of Javanese and Balinese, are indigenous Balinese narrative poems associated with the post-Majapahit era. Their subjects are the romances and battles of idealized, semi-fictional princely warriors such as the celebrated Panji. Kidung were composed in the palaces of the courts and in former times performed there by specialists in their interpretation; today there are still specialists and the music can be heard sung chorally by groups of worshippers at almost any type of Balinese ceremony.

Kidung poetic meters, called *sekar madya* (madya=medium), generally consist of pairs of double stanzas of unequal length. One characteristic type, *Rara Kadiri*, contains two stanzas of 80 syllables each, each ending with the vowel *a*, followed by two of 33 syllables, each ending with *i* (Wallis 1981:176). The vocal interpretation of kidung has historically been a confusing and difficult issue both foreign and Balinese scholars. In general the poems are sung melismatically, proceeding slowly from syllable to syllable, with a much wider melodic range than *kakawin*. Kidung is of additional historical interest because at one time its performance was accompanied by the sacred gamelan selunding, gambang and luang, a connection that suggests a former integration of vocal and gamelan music on the island.

Geguritan is a poetic genre composed in Kawi or Balinese, with texts that are topical and far less connected to elite traditions than kidung. The meters used, called *pupuh* or *tembang*, are shorter and simpler than those of other poetry. Originating in Java, and known there as *tembang macapat* (or *sekar alit*), their presence on Bali predates that of kidung. They are very widespread, all the more so in the recent past because they are central to the performance of arja theater, a twentieth century form combining story, dance and singing. In arja, as in other Balinese theatrical genres, songs are associated with specific moods and character types. The actor-dancers must also be accomplished tembang singers.

Tembang meters are of many classifications, of which seven are in general use. Each has a fixed number of lines, syllables per line, and vowel ending for each line. Stanzaic forms have from 6-9 lines, and most lines have 8, 12 or 14 syllables. Singing style is throaty and highly ornamented with melisma, quick vibrato, and glissando. The gamelan *geguntangan*, used since the early 1900s to accompany arja performances, has drums, bamboo slit-gongs (*guntang*), and a suling as its only melodic instrument. Suling players are capable of nearly as much flexibility as the singers themselves and are expected to modify their playing to match singers' choice of intonations. These may vary from moment to moment due to improvisation or dramatic requirements. Among the most famous singers of pupuh are Ni Nyoman Canderi of Singapadu village and Cokorda Isteri Rai Partini of Peliatan.

In the past twenty years there has been renewed interest in the singing of poetry. Most villages now have special groups for the study and performance of kekawin and kidung at ceremonies, and children are especially encouraged to join. There are even competitions to choose the groups with the best technique and deportment. In addition, composers have recently created gamelan forms (gegitaan and sandya gita) that integrate the singing of texts into new instrumental compositions. Many such pieces are arranged for soloists and chorus with gamelan gong kebyar, and included in the annual Festival Gong competitions.

There is plentiful vocal music that does not fit any of the categories just described, including children's songs and song-games (see Chapter 7) and songs used to accompany exorcist trance ceremonies and dances (*gending sanghyang*). The latter, heard mostly in northeastern Bali Aga villages where such ceremonies likely originated, appear to be among the oldest types of music—of any kind—on the island.

Young musicians learn social skills and concentration by mastering gamelan techniques.

CHAPTER SEVEN

Music in Balinese Society

JUST east of Rendang, a village in Karangasem district on the way to Besakih temple, there is a southward turnoff that leads onto a gravelly, unpaved road. The terrain is fairly flat but it rains almost every day in this part of Bali, and after a downpour the mud makes everything slippery. The three or four kilometer ride down the path to the village of Segah is treacherous on such days, and the village, once reached, does not extend any overt greetings to visitors. Tin roofs, scraggly dogs, a soccer field, and a few idlers chatting over coffee at a roadside stand all seem insignificant below the breathtaking vista of Mount Agung, which towers imposingly to the north.

At the south end of the village, under an open pavilion with a thatched roof and cement floor, a gamelan is rehearsing. The instrument cases, never having been carved for lack of funds and painted in swaths of brilliant red and green, have been fairly well devoured by termites, although the bronze keys and gongs sound good. The musicians, 30 of them or so, are dressed in T-shirts and woven sarongs. They are hemmed in on all sides by gawkers who crowd in so close that the players around the edges can barely move their mallets. Even though the musicians and the watchers work in the same ricefields together, those that belong to the gamelan group acquire a special aura when they make music that makes them worthy of their co-villagers prolonged stares of fascination and appreciation.

In the middle sits Windha, a composer teaching the group a new piece that they have requested from him. It is now 4 p.m. and he has been working with them without a break since 11 in the morning, going bit by bit through the music, starting at the beginning and adding more as the players can absorb it. He is patient and exacting but the music is full of complex melodies, kotekans and drumming. The piece is beautiful and intricately patterned in a way that sets the ordinariness of the villagers learning it in sharp and surprising relief. The musicians, down to the last player, are in a state of rapt concentration, and even though Windha does not assert himself very aggressively there is order, cooperation and discipline at the rehearsal. Nevertheless, some passages just prove to be too hard. The spell breaks when the reyong players make a noticeable mistake, and chaos ensues. Some continue playing heedlessly, others wipe their brows in resignation and then launch into an entirely different part of the piece, still more yell at each other in a crossfire of criticisms and exasperated complaints. Windha sits quietly in the center and gives a time-out sign.

"Ning no *ning* nong, *ni* nong ni *no* ning no *ning*," he sings, "Keep the tempo steady on the reyong!"

The reyong players try it again and again, failing utterly. All eyes are upon them. At first they are embarrassed and simper, but soon they collapse in each other's arms, laughing hysterically at themselves. They have everyone's sympathy now, so the tension abates.

"What's my part in the intro to the gangsa kotekan?" one of the jegogan players interjects. Windha demonstrates on the instrument closest to him. The jegogan players copy him, and soon the gangsa section enters with the kotekan. The reyong, meantime, is still intent on perfecting the passage they were working on, and the drummers have begun to argue over the details of one of their rhythms. The din quickly becomes unbearable.

"Quiet", says Windha in an unusually forceful tone, "Let's take it again from the beginning."

Balinese Musical Organizations

The atmosphere at the rehearsal in Segah typifies that of rehearsals that take place all the time in any of the thousands of Balinese villages with active game-lans. By dint of concentrated effort, Balinese musicians learn an art of technical rigor and esthetic power, aid in fulfilling the ritual needs of a community totally dependent on the proper placation of its deities, and play a vital role in civic life. Almost never do they earn any substantial income from music. Being a musician is primarily a voluntary public activity, centered around a communal space: the *balai banjar*, or community meeting hall. Here is where the instruments are kept, where the group meets and rehearses, and in many instances, where it performs too. People gather at the balai banjar to play gamelan for the pleasure of working hard together with their co-villagers to make something artistically satisfying and then enjoying the pride and sense of accomplishment of having done so. Making music without the challenges and rewards of group effort would be considered a pointless and unfulfilling chore to a Balinese.

The gamelan organization is only one of a roster of formally established groups, or *sekaha* (pronounced s'-kha), that operate out of each banjar. Some are a part of every banjar's organization and mandate the participation of at least one person from many of the households in the community, such as the rice harvest-ing sekaha. Others vary from village to village, are entirely voluntary, and are often so whimsical in purpose that one wonders why there is a need for any kind of formal structure or charter such as the banjar demands, like the kite flying sekaha. Why, one might ask, can't the people who like to fly kites just get together if the wind is blowing? It's just not right, and not nearly as enjoyable, answer the Balinese, unless there's a sekaha. The matrix of sekahas stipulates each individual's role in the life of the banjar and shapes the varied personalities in the community into a single, complex, functioning whole.

Whether or not the nature of Balinese music developed from these social circumstances or the circumstances were influenced by the music is moot. In any case they are ideally suited for one another. The close coordination between the gamelan's melodic parts and the interlocking of the kotekans demand a close interaction between the players during rehearsal that is analogous to the larger structure of the society. The music requires a collective memory and a group instinct that is a natural outgrowth of the musicians' proximity to each other in daily life. *Gotong royong*, the practice of mutual help, comes first, and good music follows naturally.

Belonging to the gamelan sekaha is a highly coveted privilege. As many as 75 people may take part, although only half of those can be accommodated as players at any one time. Others are understudies, administrators, instrument maintainers, treasurers, and costume designers. When wealthy businessmen in Banjar Kalah, at the south end of Peliatan village, contributed a gamelan to the banjar organization in March 1989, over 80 people signed up to join the sekaha immediately. Rehearsals had to be planned in shifts for a while so that everyone got a chance to play. A natural filtering-out process ensued in which those with greater enthusiasm and talent sought out permanent places in the ensemble; others dropped out or found other ways to be part of the sekaha. Before a premiere performance was even envisioned, a group of teenage boys threw themselves into the week-long production of an elaborate stage backdrop for the instruments. Give a new gamelan to a banjar, and watch the community come glowingly to life.

Teachers and the Learning Process

When a banjar acquires a gamelan it does two things right away: set up the administrative apparatus to support a sekaha, and search for an auspicious day on the Balinese calendar to have the gamelan blessed and activities inaugurated. Once this is taken care of, a teacher must be procured, for the group cannot proceed without one. If there is no one knowledgeable within the banjar, arrangements are made for an outsider to be brought in.

If the teacher is a performing member of the group, he sits himself behind the lead drum at rehearsals. If not, he takes a place in the center that is visible to all. To start he approaches one of the gangsas in the front row and plays through a section of the piece to be taught, gesturing the gongs and kempli into motion at the right times. Before he has even played a few notes, the group begins to imitate him—blindly and cacophonously at first, but after a while the sound comes into focus. The musicians learn both by listening to what he plays and, just as importantly, by watching the direction his mallet takes across the keys. They memorize the music as a group, instinctively reacting to and correcting each other. After some time, the teacher moves over to the reyong and drums

The teacher demonstrates the melodies and patterns to be learned on the intrument closest to him.

and demonstrates their parts. As the music cycles around, the core melody instruments can usually derive their own parts from what the gangsas play. If individual players are having trouble they are given special attention, or simply allowed to falter on the assumption that, in time, the music will 'enter them'.

A brand new group needs time to master the technique of damping the keys. To this end, a simple piece like a gilak ostinato may be played over and over again for days or weeks until the sound is clear and articulate. An established group, experienced in learning together, may bite off a substantial chunk of music at a sitting, spending most of the rehearsal time working out details of dynamics, tempo and angsel. Before long they can play even the most demanding music with verve and conviction.

It is impossible to imagine gamelan players reading from a musical score or parts the way Western musicians do, even though it is quite possible to write the music down. Reading music is a process of translating symbols into sounds; Balinese musicians bypass this stage entirely and learn music by transforming a received musical gesture directly into the physical act of playing. Correspondingly, the variety of different kinds of musical patterns, while infinite, is not quite as infinite as it is in Western music. Although each piece is unique, the instruments each have their roles, melodies have recognizable forms, and there are only so many different styles of kotekan. This partially explains how Balinese musicians can memorize such great amounts of music. On the other hand, there is no explanation for the breadth of some players' memories. Many can access any of hundreds of tunes and their accompanying parts, some of which they may not have recalled for years, in a brief instant.

A new gamelan's first task is to learn the repertoire of lelambatan needed for temple ceremonies, for a sekaha's central purpose is to fulfill ritual needs. Simultaneously they will learn the music needed to accompany the *topeng* (masked dance) play as this also has religious associations. Then it is up to the group to decide which, if any, kinds of secular music appeal to them, taking into account the types of performances that are likely to generate some income for the sekaha treasury. Gamelans without such ambitious plans will learn enough repertoire to be able to provide unremunerated entertainment within their own village when it is called for. In South Bali, however, many sekaha assemble tari lepas performances in the hope of procuring a regular, paying engagement playing for tourists. In outlying areas it can be profitable to hook up with a company of actors and singers to perform the perennially popular *drama gongs*, given with full musical accompaniment, that Balinese audiences flock to see. When a sekaha does earn money, only a very insignificant percentage, if any, goes into the players' pockets. Most goes into the treasury. The members earn their sustenance from other jobs, complementing it with the recognition and satisfaction that comes from being part of a gamelan group.

Teachers are rarely paid in cash; Balinese find it awkward or inappropriate to attempt to fix a monetary value for the transmission of musical knowledge. The process of payment is instead much more complex and involves establishing a relationship that cannot be neatly terminated once the teacher completes his professional obligations to the group. For years to come the group members will shower special favors on him, bringing foodstuffs to his home before a feast or providing a team of carpenters and free labor if part of his home needs renovation. Many teachers will beam with pride in explaining that they have never once been so crass as to ask for any kind of payment, and then go on to describe all the various kinds of compensation that have been voluntarily given by students in expression of their gratitude and respect.

Children and Music

Children in Bali begin their musical education at an early age. Since gamelan instruments are kept in the balai banjar, they are accessible not just to the members of the sekaha, but to the community at large. When rehearsals take place they are open to all, and children are encouraged to attend. Those who have a parent playing in the group can often be seen sitting on their fathers' laps watching and listening intently. Others crowd around the edge of the rehearsal space. After rehearsal and during the mornings, kids return to bang out their own improvisational approximations of what they have heard. No parent ever directs their child to study music or to take lessons, and there are no scales to practice or exercises to master. It is not necessary to purchase an instrument for home study or to make any kind of investment. Children who evince a serious interest simply

Children begin their musical education in informal imitation of their elders.

progress on their own from crude mimicking to careful imitation to the thorough absorption of the actual repertoire, all of which is solidly reinforced by constant exposure to the adult group's music making.

In addition to nurturing physical dexterity and sensitive musicianship, as a large group activity gamelan is also an ideal laboratory for developing discipline, cooperation and other social skills that will go a long way towards helping young Balinese grow into productive members of their society. As an educational environment there is little that could surpass it. When young Balinese learn music, they also come into contact with dance, theater, puppetry, mythology and literature, experiencing through direct participation the matrix of artistic activities that their traditional life cultivates. Even at the youngest of ages they are made aware of the great importance attached to music. From birth onward babies are feted with a series of prescribed religious ceremonies that utilize gamelan, and soon thereafter they become aware of the continuous presence of gamelan at ceremonies of all kinds, both within the temples and without. When they are old enough to want to try the instruments out for themselves, there is no discouragement, intimidation, or inference that making music is an activity reserved for a privileged few. There are only the instruments, other similarly inclined playmates, and the beginnings of the life-long practice of the music itself.

Music is often a family affair. Some families have artistic blood going back for generations and even venerate their inherited talent with a special shrine for *taksu* (performance charisma) in their temple. Children in these homes are flooded with musical stimuli from birth and are often expert drummers or gender players from an early age. The sense of dedication is terrific: one drummer from Denpasar talks of having taken his drum to bed with him every night during his childhood, waking up each morning to begin the day by practicing before a mirror to refine posture and facial expression. Now he, along with three brothers and sisters, are among the best known musicians in Bali.

In the 1930s, Colin McPhee presented a gamelan angklung to the children in the village of Sayan. He wrote about their rapid evolution from being a bunch of ordinary children to being in demand as a serious organization of skilled musicians in A Club of Small Men and "Children and Music in Bali". Today organized children's sekaha are commonplace. It is uncanny to witness the earnestness and precision with which such groups, made up of children ages 7-17, play the same difficult pieces that their elders play. Some young musicians are barely able to get their hands around both ends of a drum before they can perform with an assurance that belies their age.

Very young Balinese have their own musical domain in the *dolanan*, or children's songs and song-games, of which there are hundreds. Some of these are found Bali-wide; others are known only in certain villages or regions. There are nonsense songs, clapping games, lullabies, and melodies with movements or activities tied to them. As is true nearly everywhere, television and radio are having their deleterious effect on the popularity of these songs, but they are still an important pastime and a good way of learning social and musical skills for Bali's children.

Recent Developments

Until very recently the only place for women in Balinese musical life was either as a singer—in the temple or as a character actress in a dramatic performance— or as a performer in the informal *oncang-oncangan*, a kind of music made from the interlocking sounds of bamboo poles striking the ground during rice husking. Women's roles in traditional artistic life were generally restricted to dancing, weaving and the making of offerings. Men monopolized the plastic arts of painting and carving, shared the dance stage with women, and played gamelan.

During the past decade there have been some changes. In 1979 the first women puppeteers performed, and at around the same time a few female music majors enrolled at the conservatory. Two of these, Ketut Suryatini and Desak Made Laksmi, joined the faculty after they graduated. In the mid-1980s the first all-female gong kebyar sekaha were founded and included, along with men's gamelans, into the yearly Festival Gong gamelan competitions. In keeping with the regulations of the festival, every year a different group from each of Bali's eight districts must enter, so that by now several dozen women's gamelans have been formed. Some disband soon after the competitions, having no ambitions beyond the goal of competing. Others, such as the women's group in Peliatan village, grow into mature organizations that maintain a regular performance schedule.

The experience of playing gamelan is as new for the women doing it as it is for the people who come to see it. Thus far there have not been any mixed-gender groups, but as the notion of women musicians becomes more familiar, some may emerge. These sorts of changes take root slowly. The women's groups are of secular origin and hence have not penetrated the surface of the Balinese social structure. If they do, girls will receive the same encouragement to play music in the banjar that boys do, and women's musicianship will be cultivated in a vital way, incorporated into the communal and religious life of the village.

The gamelan competitions which lately have been the primary forum for women musicians have long been a fixture in Balinese musical life. The first ones were held every few years during the 30s and 40s; recently they have been taking place every May and June without fail. In March or early April, the eight regional governments each select one women's and one men's group from their district as representatives. Teams of locally-based coaches and teachers are sent to the chosen villages regularly to help with the rehearsals, which commence upon a group's selection and continue daily for two months. Competition guidelines clearly delineate what must be prepared: One lelambatan, one kreasi baru instrumental piece, two classical dances, one new choreography, and one choral piece with full gamelan accompaniment. Then in late May, a committee of experts is sent by the government arts council to see a full rehearsal and give suggestions and comments.

During the first two weeks of June the competition is held. The atmosphere at these events is much more reminiscent of a sporting event than a concert. Outside the performance area vendors set up all manner of wares from coffee and cakes to toys from Hong Kong. The crowd overflows from the auditorium, usually a roofed pavilion with no walls, and spills out into the streets and up palm trees and walls. The audiences are thoroughly responsive to everything taking place in the music or dance, reacting instantaneously with approving cheers at a particularly well-executed passage, or jeering with abandon at the slightest mistake. (At one such concert in Amlapura in 1977, a missed jegogan tone brought 3,000 people to their feet in a spontaneous chorus of boos.) Through the hubbub, the jury members calmly make notes on their little pads, voting on 1st and 2nd place winners once they have seen all of the performances. The four winners, two women's and two men's groups, carry their torches of glory to the Denpasar Art Center, where they perform at the Bali Arts Festival in late June or early July.

The yearly Festival Gong and Bali Arts Festival, the constant stream of musical performances emanating from the conservatories, and the ever-increasing number of village sekaha with regular work performing for tourists, have created a broader range of contexts for gamelan in secular life than has heretofore been known in Bali. This has often had the effect of strengthening the sacred ties which are the root of the tradition, simply because there are more sekaha available and eager to play their part in rituals.

At the same time, many young Balinese, bombarded by a hail of outside influences resulting from Indonesia's increasing international presence, and the influx of tourists, foreign goods and Western culture, are perhaps less aware than ever of the history and diversity of their own music. As one journalist wrote in the Bali Post recently, "Ask a young teenager in Denpasar the meaning of the terms Semar Pegulingan, gong gde or gambuh and they will shrug their shoulders in ignorance." While that may be something of an exaggeration, it is certainly indicative of the struggle that a dynamic and changing society like Bali's must undergo in order to maintain its identity in the late 20th century.

I Wayan Tembres

CHAPTER EIGHT

Three Generations
of Balinese Musicians

I N Bali individual musicians rarely emerge as stars in their own right. The
interlocking, cooperative levels of Balinese society and their reflection in
the making of music work to discourage this. On the whole it is the sekaha
that achieve recognition, especially those that have noteworthy accomplish-
ments to their credit, have attained a markedly high level of musicianship, or are
the preservers of an unusual style or form. Yet players of extraordinary ability and
personality do gain a certain fame as teachers and disseminators. Bali is small
enough to ensure that their numbers are comparatively few and their milieus
interconnected. The tone of Balinese musical life is set by this intimate community, whose members circulate among the village groups of the island directing,
coaching and lending their expertise whenever their skills are requested. The
efforts and aspirations of these artists make them the role models that younger
Balinese musicians look up to. Their work steers a course for the development
and regeneration of the tradition.

The three musicians profiled in the following pages have been chosen with
difficulty since so many of their gifted colleagues had to be excluded. As a trio they
represent a cross-section of the musical community in terms of age, experience
and outlook. All are active today and affiliated with a village or institution that
has been important in the recent development of Balinese music. The first one, I
Wayan Tembres, represents the increasingly rare breed of unschooled and thoroughly traditional musicians that have made their lives in music as teachers and
performers in village groups. The second, I Made Bandem, is an influential academic with an international reputation at the peak of his career. Lastly, I Wayan
Rai, who grew up at a time when attendance at the conservatory had already
been accepted as the natural path for a serious young musician to take, sets forth
his opinions about the role of traditional music in contemporary Balinese life.

I Wayan Tembres

As one of the senior statesmen of Balinese gamelan, Wayan Tembres personifies
the village teacher. Carrying on the time-honored practice of offering his skills to
villages desirous of forming or improving a sekaha, Tembres has, during the past
fifty years, established a broad network of disciples and colleagues throughout the

island. Cheerfully contradicting the archetype of the venerable and inscrutable guru, Tembres is playful, witty, humble, and possesses a burning musical energy. Although nearing 70, he has the spirit of a man half his age.

Tembres is from Blangsinga, about 1 kilometer south of Blahbatuh village. With its heritage of courtly arts, this culturally vibrant region provided a fertile environment for his training. Like most aspiring musicians in Bali, Tembres hardly ever had one-to-one study with elder musicians. Rather he learned by tagging along with his father Pareg, a rebab and suling player at the court (right up until his death in 1991 at over 90 years of age, he made hand-carved suling daily), and by absorbing and imitating the music he heard all around him.

Best known as a drummer with an incisive attack and unwavering rhythm, his presence at the helm of a gamelan inspires calm and assurance in his fellow musicians and brings out verve and intensity in dancers. Tembres' most famous students are the sekaha from Pindha village (see page 80), on the road south of Blangsinga. During the 60s, he steered them towards their participation and near-triumph in the 1969 Festival Gong. The event was one of the climactic points of his career:

"I was scheduled to play drum for Pindha against the Geladag group at an amphitheater in Bangli. That day I had been taken to Denpasar by motorbike to arrange my official papers for a gamelan tour to Teheran that I was departing with the next week. On the way back to Bangli we had an accident. I passed out and came to disoriented and bloody. Nevertheless I insisted on getting to the performance area so I could formally request permission not to play. But when I got there the group wouldn't hear of it; they were scared to go on without me. I was covered with bandages but I had to acquiesce. It was my condition that caused me to miss some key angsels that night, and the audience practically rioted on account of my mistakes. The whole situation was out of control, but I kept playing. The jury had to give us second place but I got plenty of recognition for my endurance and dedication.

"The Pindha group was and is very strong. I can be critical and even show some anger when I work with them because they already have the skills they need and should not shirk from applying those skills. They are disciplined and absolutely uniform and that is the key to playing well. But I believe that in teaching beginners one must cajole, joke, and above all be patient. Once they know the music, then you can proceed in earnest. That's where the real work begins.

"Music entails being sensitive to signals from musicians, dancers, and especially from the audience. The drummer can use his craft to enliven any performance at which the audience shows signs of boredom. If the dancer is acting forlorn, cue a few surprise angsels! If the musicians' concentration wavers, pull up the tempo a bit. That snaps them back to attention every time.

"I taught myself to play the kendang by listening to other players and figuring out what they did as best I could. But finally I had to create my own style. The village atmosphere is good for that kind of learning. Students who now do well at

KOKAR and STSI should remember that they could never have made it there without the kind of training they got at home.

"Some things are more difficult for musicians now than they used to be, and some are better. When I was young school and outside pressures were not present to keep my friends and me from playing music all day every day. Now, obviously, it's harder for young people to find that much time for gamelan, unless they enter a conservatory. But the ones that are serious play very well. Music is just as well-performed today as it ever was.

"I have never asked for money as a teacher. It's not right to do so. The rewards come to you anyhow, in other ways. We get a token fee for performing in the hotels now that we never used to get, but it's not enough for anyone to consider that a reason for doing those performances. We do them for the activity and the challenge, and for the strength of the sekaha organization. In the temples, of course, it's our duty to play for free and it always will be. No one fails to meet those obligations, and that's why our tradition is so strong."

Dr. Made Bandem

Foremost among Bali's cultural disseminators is Dr. Made Bandem, head of the STSI academy in Denpasar. Bandem's guidance has been essential to the development of the school ever since its founding in the 1960s. Trained primarily as a dancer, but also skilled as a musician and very active as a scholar, Bandem's influence is strongly felt not only within the school but throughout the island and amongst ethnomusicologists worldwide.

Bandem was born in 1945. His father, the late I Made Keredek, was a renowned dancer and literary scholar from Singapadu village. During the first half of the 20th century Keredek was instrumental in the development of several important theatrical forms, supporting his creativity with a pronounced intellectual energy that his son thoroughly absorbed. As a member of one of the conservatories' first graduating classes, Bandem was involved in the inception of the *sendratari* music/dance/drama form, a performance genre that has since demonstrated a staying power and ability to absorb influences of other styles akin to kebyar in its vitality. He performed widely during his youth as a dancer and was a member of several cultural missions abroad, including one to Beijing in 1963. He spent much of the late 60s and 70s as a student in the United States, ultimately obtaining a Ph.D. in ethnomusicology from Wesleyan University.

The rapid ascendance of STSI as a center for Balinese music and dance and the larger questions that arise when the school's pivotal role in the overall cultural scene are examined form the core of Bandem's commentary on his work and aspirations:

"The Balinese are a very tolerant and creative people. What this in effect means for our performing arts is that absorption of outside influences and internal growth move at a rate much too quick for us to document and codify completely. Each generation of musicians in our society will have a markedly dif-

Dr. Made Bandem

ferent history from its predecessors and successors. We are very fast to learn but never satisfied to simply receive knowledge as presented; we feel compelled to interpret and modify it. At STSI and elsewhere we can record, videotape and write about changes in our music with diligence and thoroughness, but none of these activities have the same intrinsic value as the kind of living documentation— namely, the very process of learning, creating and performing our music— that needs to be emphasized most.

"I am aware of how distinct our creative process is from that of the West, and I like these differences very much. In the West there is a focus on the individual and the potential for unique and original artistry. In Bali what we have is a shared pool of cultural resources that all of our artists tap into and take from instinctively. We don't really have breaks with the past or drastic changes, instead we have transformation, ornamentation, development. Almost all of our new music is based on classical models. This is an important concept.

"For the greater part of our recorded history we have been isolated in Bali. For almost 500 years no one disturbed us. Our kings and our gods were unquestioned sources of authority and wisdom and the benevolent presiders over the growth of our arts. Hindu culture was preserved and confined in Bali and to this day the Balinese do not want to change this any more than is necessary. They have been peaceful and feel no need to revolutionize or sever ties.

"Kebyar is still developing and will probably not decline in popularity for some time to come because of its musical flexibility and the freedom with which it can be used. Seven-tone and other older gamelans may revive but all of these have specific ritual connotations whereas kebyar from the very first was intended exclusively for artistic presentation. There were over 1500 active kebyar groups in Bali the last time the Ministry of Culture took a census, and there are probably more that are dormant. The profusion is delightful.

"We have a responsibility at STSI to be involved in the upholding of artistic standards, particularly where tourist performances are concerned. Many groups are overworked—some perform nightly—and are not always able to do their best. We're initiating a program to have our students and graduates help to organize the village groups and negotiate on their behalf with hotel managers for reasonable performance schedules. We would also like to see some graduates employed as artistic directors at the hotels themselves, where they would organize the music and dance programs and work to educate visitors about what is presented.

"There are more musicians in Bali now that think of themselves as professionals in a way that was not so in the past. These artists are well positioned to play a major role in our international relations. I believe that many will be able to earn their livelihood from music before long. We will have more cultural missions and teachers going abroad, study programs for foreign students, gamelans shipped overseas—all of which makes our musicians proud and gives them work too! Cultural exchange raises the musi-

I Wayan Rai

cians' quality of life and by example provides motivation for younger generations.

"There is nothing that Bali is more proud of than her arts, and music and dance are the most expressive of these. Through them, Westerners will know the Balinese mind, soul and personality. They will be our connection to the rest of the world. And since music has universal meanings as well as culturally specific ones, no one will deny us our pride. Rather, they will seek to understand us better."

I Wayan Rai

I Wayan Rai, or Pak Rai as he is called, is at the center of the musical renaissance that has overtaken the village of Ubud recently. He was born on May 26, 1955 just a few houses north of the center of town into a non-musical family, but his aptitude for gamelan was apparent from his boyhood. In those days there were many active gamelans among Ubud's 12 banjars, and whenever they rehearsed or performed Rai was there listening and imitating in the manner of all would-be Balinese musicians.

Rai refined his skills in Junior High School, where he played ugal for the school gamelan club. By this time his ambitions were apparent, so he pursued a musical education, attending SMKI and STSI conservatories in Bali and eventually, in 1986, completing an M.A. in Ethnomusicology at San Diego State University in the United States. He is now on the STSI faculty and juggles a variety of pursuits, including teaching a number of different gamelan styles, compiling a collection of dolanan (children's songs), making a bibliography of writings about Balinese music, composing and performing newly commissioned works, leading research field trips for students, and administering the foreign students program at STSI. His wife, Gusti Ayu Srinatih, is from Tabanan district. She is a dancer and also an STSI graduate. They have two young sons, Degus and Indra.

For nearly a decade Rai has supervised musical activities in his home village, to which he feels a keen sense of dedication. During his youth Rai witnessed an extreme decline in Ubud's musical life, most of which was accountable to severe intra-banjar rivalries resulting from the political turmoil that shook Indonesia in the 50s and 60s, most notably in the aftermath of the 1965 coup attempt. By the late 70s, Ubud's banjars were quiet and attendance at temple ceremonies was sloppy and lackluster. Music in the surrounding area was virtually restricted to the neighboring village of Peliatan, which had dominated the scene for decades with its internationally famous gong kebyar group. In 1980, a gamelan competition to include groups from Ubud and the surrounding villages was proposed, but Ubud nearly walked out because tensions were so high and musicianship so low that coordinators were stumped by the difficulty of choosing a sekaha to represent the village. As Rai describes it, the situation filled him with shame, and he felt compelled to initiate some changes:

"I thought it would be a good idea to create a kind of all-star sekaha by picking a few representatives from each banjar to form a new group. All of the village leaders supported me in this and my musician friends from Junior High School were anxious to help too. We founded Gamelan Sadha Budaya—*sadha* meaning 12, for Ubud's 12 banjars, and *budaya* meaning culture—and rehearsed two or three times a day in preparation for the competition. The contest ended without a decision, but we were not disappointed because our primary goal was not so much to compete as it was to revitalize things. As we hoped, the members of Sadha Budaya took their rekindled enthusiasm back to their own banjars and used it to reawaken the spirit of music making throughout the village.

"But I saw this as just the beginning of a larger process. After all, the source of our musical culture is in the ceremonies and temples, and in Ubud those had become pretty drab and uninspired. I knew that I had to cultivate music for rituals in order for gamelan to truly take root in Ubud again, and I knew that the impetus had to come from young people. Too many of Ubud's teenagers were spending a lot of time loitering and riding their motorbikes. Playing music in the temple seemed old-fashioned and a waste of time to them and for their younger brothers and sisters this attitude was infectious, unfortunately.

"I started by teaching sacred ceremonial dances like *Baris Gde* and *Rejang* to small children. We had few resources and had to borrow costumes for the first performance, but we preceded it with a great procession to the temple which everyone came out to see. I think we really touched people that day and made them see the potential for traditional music and dance in our village. Soon offers of help were coming in from all the parents. Many contributed funds, especially those making extra money from tourism, and we were able to buy everything we needed. Excitement was building and the temples were packed for ceremonies. This made me—and all of Ubud—very happy.

"Now with their parents and kid brothers and sisters involved, the teenagers were embarrassed not to be a part of things. I figured that they needed some discipline and direction for their energies so I helped them get organized into sekaha in their banjars. It has been surprising to see that they are the most enthusiastic musicians of all—chasing down their friends when they are late for rehearsal and busily raising funds for new costumes and instruments.

"Music in Ubud is really alive these days. There is an active gamelan in nearly every one of the 12 banjars and a performance somewhere in town every night of the week. Sadha Budaya continues to play; they recently toured Japan and Germany with a brand new 7-tone gamelan purchased with the help of Cokorda Putera, a descendant of the Ubud royal family. Most of the performances in town are for tourists, but now the general attitude is that if you're not active in the temples then you're just a money-grabber and not a true musician.

"Tourism has both positive and negative effects, obviously, but in general I think it has mainly been beneficial. Of course Westerners have been present in Ubud since the 30s, when [the painters] Walter Spies and Rudolf Bonnet were here commissioning performances and encouraging new ideas. The situation is basically the same now, just a lot more developed. Not long ago a group of tourists wanted to see a certain kind of performance that was not playing in Ubud, so they brought in a group from somewhere else. That got some of our people incensed, and within a week they had formed their own club to learn to do it themselves. The negatives are there too, of course, but they have more to do with things like clothing and lifestyle. Balinese kids are often really quick to imitate the fashions and manners of some visitors, which are mostly not appropriate for Bali.

"The most important thing is to begin music and dance education at an early age and continue it. This is true not only in Ubud but all over Bali. Balinese have to cultivate *ngayah*—devotion and community work. I must be active in helping to preserve these values. We will feel deeply satisfied if we live with this in mind, because if our arts and culture are ever lost, what then?

"I hope that foreigners will have a chance to learn about our culture before and during their stays here so that they will be able to appreciate Balinese arts with a more critical eye. The more they come out to the villages to see gamelans play the better. That kind of interaction is good for all of us. I would like to be of help to anyone looking for such experiences. Most mornings I'm at STSI and am happy to receive visitors there."

Gamelan gender wayang batel at a temple ceremony in Mas village.

CHAPTER NINE

Getting Involved

BALINESE music is a tradition of extraordinary vitality and a source of pride for the Balinese. The centuries of cultural isolation that Bali experienced prior to the 20th century served to fortify the social and religious roles of gamelan music to such an extent that the rapid influx of foreign ideas that besiege Bali today are perceived mostly as a valuable stimulus to musical development rather than as a threat. In no way can it be said that the tradition is ossified; in fact, as we have seen, there is more music and musical creativity in Bali today than ever before.

As recently as a few decades ago only only the most progressive of Western musicians sought direct interaction with other musical cultures. With the exception of a handful of ethnographers, most Westerners exposed to gamelan music in the past experienced it as an exotic phenomenon and did not pursue it beyond that. Of course, the music was not nearly as accessible then as it is today. Now hundreds of thousands of visitors come to Bali yearly and hear gamelan music as a matter of course during their stay. Among them are many foreign students who come with the express purpose of learning to play gamelan instruments either in the villages from local teachers or, more formally, at one of the conservatories. Gamelans from Bali perform abroad regularly and many sets of instruments have found their way to other countries, where interested people study the music either from experienced non-Balinese or directly from native teachers. Balinese musicians teaching abroad may be part of the Indonesian diplomatic service or they may, as is sometimes the case with conservatory faculty, be pursuing advanced degrees in ethnomusicology or a related subject at foreign universities.

For Balinese musicians involved in such developments, these are encouraging processes that merit full support. As Dr. Bandem noted in the previous chapter, the arts are the primary medium through which the Balinese hope to establish a meaningful connection with the world at large. Foreigners who evince an interest in gamelan music are therefore met with respect and appreciation by musicians on the island. Such interactions are tangible proof of the esteem in which gamelan music is held internationally, which in turn further reinforces the importance of cultivating the music for the Balinese themselves.

Offerings are made before every performance.

Musical Performances

Most foreigners who arrive in Bali for a brief stay encounter gamelan in performance at hotels. There are many sekaha whose home villages are situated in reasonable proximity to tourist-concentrated areas that have regular contractual engagements to offer a selection of music and dance pieces on stages set up at the hotels themselves; others perform daily or weekly in their villages at balai banjars outfitted with chairs and lighting for a bussed-in audience. All of these performances are regulated by the government arts council LISTIBIYA, which auditions and certifies the groups for quality and authenticity.

Most programs of this type offer an opening instrumental composition followed by a welcoming dance, derived from a sacred temple dance, in which pairs of female dancers make offerings and strew the audience with flower petals as a gesture of greeting. Thereupon follows a mixed selection of tari lepas kebyar-style dances, some classical masked dances or a Baris, and perhaps even a Legong. Some groups, notably the ones that perform in Batubulan village, present more elaborate theatrical pieces that involve the protector-dragon Barong and its nemesis, the witch Rangda. This last, which is extremely sacred in origin and fraught with dangerous magical connotations in its original temple setting, has been altered and condensed so as to render it appropriate for recreational presentation. Nevertheless, before these and all gamelan performances, a priest is summoned to bless the performance area, musicians, dancers and instruments, and to propitiate any malevolent forces that might conspire to disrupt or otherwise adversely affect the presentation.

Groups engaged to perform in hotels are usually hired for a set fee, out of which musicians' and dancers' honorariums and other expenses including costumes, maintenance and transportation must be paid. The performers end up with very little in their pockets—normally less than US $1 per performance—but the steadiness of the work does provide a supplement to whatever other sources of income they have. On performance days a truck is hired and at about 6 p.m. the sekaha members appear on the roadside in their village waiting to be picked up. They load the heavy gamelan instruments into the bed of the truck, pile in with it and head towards the hotel, their multi-colored musicians uniforms drawing stares and cheers from bystanders along the road.

Other Venues for Hearing Music

While hotel performances are mostly of high quality, they can only give an inkling of the experience that Balinese music offers in its natural environment at temples in villages around the island. Temple anniversary ceremonies, known as *odalans*, are almost always underway somewhere. Visitors are welcome and encouraged to attend these events, with the essential stipulations that full Balinese temple dress be worn and that the progress of the ceremony not be disturbed. (Most any Balinese contact, guide or hotel employee can provide information on where odalans are taking place at any given time and give instruction on matters of clothing and etiquette.) The best time to hear music at a temple ceremony is in the late afternoon and early evening, when offerings are brought in to the accompaniment of lelambatan, gamelan angklung, or other gamelans that a village may maintain. After hours there is often a complete dance or theatrical performance or a shadow play.

For those with more time and some curiosity about the music-making process, attending a rehearsal is the best way to get an insider's view. Here there is opportunity to sit close to the musicians, hear passages repeated (which clarifies one's perception of them), and feel the physical power of the music at close range. Practices, like ceremonies, are always taking place somewhere, but it may require a bit of sleuthing to find out about them. A casual drive through back roads after dark will often lead to an illuminated balai banjar filled with musicians and instruments. During April and May Festival Gong rehearsals take place daily; these can be located by dropping by one of the music schools and asking in the faculty offices. During morning class hours, the conservatories themselves provide an excellent venue for visitors to hear and see musicians practicing. Many of the faculty speak English and all are available year round to advise people seeking out good music. STSI is located on Jalan Nusa Indah in Denpasar and KOKAR/SMKI is in Batubulan village.

If there is a particular type of music or a specific gamelan group that you wish to hear (such as one of the famous ones mentioned in Chapter 6), it is not at all impractical to commission a command performance by going to the ensemble's village and negotiating directly (perhaps with the help of an interpreter) with the *ketua sekaha gong* (head of the gamelan group). Arrangements can be made to accommodate visitors right in the village at the banjar hall or any other suitable space nearby. The price of such a performance will vary according to its length and elaborateness, so it is important to establish scope and cost fairly and firmly beforehand. In any case a group of 10 or so commissioners should find it quite affordable to hire a troupe of musicians and dancers for an evening's entertainment. Person-to-person contacts between outsiders and village artists of this sort can be very rewarding for both parties, and are likely to result in a memorable event.

A final important venue for hearing music in Bali that bears mention is the yearly Bali Arts Festival, held at the Denpasar Art Center from mid-June to mid-July. An effort is made here to present a diverse selection of classical and modern dance and music at the daily performances. On weekends, thousands of spectators cram into the Ardha Chandra open theater to witness the *sendratari* extravaganzas produced exclusively for the Festival by the conservatories and regional arts councils. Other events at the Festival range from craft exhibits to speech-making contests to academic seminars to fashion shows.

Learning Balinese Music

Any hands-on opportunity to play Balinese musical instruments can provide insight into the music not obtainable through passive listening. With this kind of direct interaction one learns not just the melodies, kotekans and instrumental techniques, but also undergoes the rote learning process, which illuminates the special teacher-student relationship and its implications for the larger role of music in Balinese life. Even just a few lessons will shed light on some of these issues. Lack of musical background or any imagined shortage of aptitude should not be thought of as obstacles, because the Balinese way of learning music involves the development of a different set of perceptive faculties than those that Western music education ordinarily stimulates, and many foreigners—even those without musical experience—find themselves naturally suited to it.

Finding a teacher is a simple matter. By speaking to musicians after a performance, inquiring around the area where you are staying, or, best yet, by making an excursion to one of the conservatories and asking the advice of faculty members, plenty of suggestions are bound to emerge. Determine first, or ask advice on, what style of music you wish to study. The most frequent choices are gong kebyar, gender wayang, and tingklik (gamelan joged bumbung). If gong kebyar is chosen, begin by learning the mallet and damping technique for the gangsa, as the main melody and the kotekan parts can both be played on it. It is less productive to begin with other instruments like the reyong or kendang; grasping their more abstract parts will be much easier once the melodies have been internalized. Lessons can take place at a balai banjar, private home, or other

To the Balinese who perform it, gamelan's connection to religion remains its most salient feature.

rehearsal space where there are a pair of instruments that can be set up facing each other. Bring a tape recorder if possible to record the material presented at the lesson for reference and practice later.

Determining appropriate payment for lessons is often a bit tricky because Balinese generally do not teach music privately. Rather all of their instruction is given in a group context and involves long term obligations that are rarely stated explicitly. At the first lesson, make some inquiries. Some teachers with experience teaching foreigners may well have established a set fee, but others will be reluctant to discuss it at all or insist that the amount of payment is entirely dependent upon the student's resources. Don't press the issue, even though it may seem unusual to engage a teacher without a prior understanding about money. Continue studying and ask other foreign students or Balinese musicians about the going rate. Hand the appropriate amount to your teacher, sealed in an envelope, at the end of your study, or, if you will be staying for some time, at intervals during it.

In longer-term situations, it is also worthwhile to consider helping your teacher with some specific need, such as contributing to the cost of home improvements. The total amount of money involved may be equivalent to what a cash payment would be, but the effect is enhanced in that such material purchases simultaneously fulfill a practical purpose and imbue your relationship with your teacher with a sense of family that is inimitably Balinese.

Students with even more ambitious aspirations can enquire at the conservatories about long-term stay permits, academic sponsorship, scholarships, and degree programs. Serious students should have some sort of connection with STSI or KOKAR/SMKI, both because of the expert advice and council available there, and because it is deemed necessary to go through official channels in such a case.

Balinese Music Abroad

A noteworthy component of the expanding interface between Bali and the rest of the world has been the appearance of a number of ensembles based in foreign countries that are devoted to the study, cultivation, and performance of Balinese gamelan on authentic instruments. Some of these groups are based at Indonesian consulates or embassies, others are at universities as part of ethnomusicology curriculums, and a small but growing number are privately owned and maintained. Most cultivate a community membership and model their organization on that of the Balinese banjar and sekaha system. These groups, along with other ones dedicating themselves to Javanese gamelan or to one of the many hybrid Western-made gamelan instruments and styles that have emerged in tandem with the growth of traditional gamelan in the West, have each played their part in raising the music's international profile.

The first Balinese gamelan to be shipped out of Indonesia for study purposes was purchased by the University of California at Los Angeles Music Department in the late 1950s, just before Colin McPhee joined the faculty there. At the time, it was considered unorthodox for students to learn about the music of another culture by actually playing its instruments. But the idea—termed "bimusicality" by ethnomusicologist Mantle Hood—caught on fast. A few years later in Indonesia, the conservatories were established, and there began a regular flow of faculty musicians and dancers going abroad to pursue advanced degrees. Thus the apparatus was in place, outside of Bali, for the formation of student ensembles directed by native masters. This has since been the model followed, whenever possible, by international gamelan groups.

Now there are hundreds of Balinese, Javanese and newly created gamelan groups of all kinds scattered worldwide. A website at *http://www.glue.umd.edu/~satu/gamelan* plus related links accessible there lists most active non-Indonesian groups and can give an idea of the concentration of international activity in this field. Indonesian-sponsored Balinese gamelans in the U.S. are situated at the embassy in Washington D.C. and at the consulates in New York and Los Angeles; a partial list of the universities that maintain them includes UCLA, California Institute of the Arts, Bowling Green State University, Brown University, Florida State University, and the University of British Columbia. Among the community groups are the Sekar Jaya of El Cerrito, California, and the Galak Tika of Cambridge, Massachusetts, New York (both gamelan gong kebyars), and a gamelan angklung in Denver, Colorado. There are active Balinese gamelans in Montreal, Canada; Belfast, Northern Ireland; Munich and Freiburg, West

Germany; Melbourne, Australia; and Tokyo, Japan. These ensembles often have busy performance schedules that feature collaborative work with guest Balinese artists. Nearly all of them, including the consular and university groups, are often on the lookout for enthusiastic new players. Information about existing or newly-formed gamelan groups can be had by contacting education and culture representatives at Indonesian consulates.

The American Sekar Jaya and the Japanese Sekar Jepun gamelan groups accepted official invitations to participate in the Bali Arts Festival in 1985 and 1987 respectively, thus becoming the first foreign ensembles to formally perform Balinese music and dance in Bali for the Balinese. Sekar Jaya undertook an extensive tour which included performances around the island in competition style with local groups, broadcasts on national television, and a concert in Java. Both they and Sekar Jepun were received with great warmth and graciousness by the public, with a tacit acknowledgement that even though neither's presentation was yet at a level with the Balinese, something of a serious beginning had been made in setting standards for the international cultivation of Balinese performing arts. Sekar Jaya returned to Bali in 1992 and 1995 to present programs of experimental and non-traditional works, which were also well-received.

Balinese music has leapt in a short time from the isolation to which it was but recently confined to the tumultuous musical arenas of our age. And it would seem that the current interaction with foreigners has also reaped some benefits. Some of these are financial, others take less concrete but no less valuable forms and are measured in education, exchange of ideas, recognition, and appreciation. To be sure, the rapidity of change in Bali has had its traumatic effects. A few older styles of music do not hold much interest for today's audiences, and some young Balinese clearly prefer Indonesian and Western pop to anything they hear in the temple. But this is neither a phenomenon that is restricted to Bali nor a potential threat to traditional music in its ongoing ritual role. The continued relevance of gamelan in the daily life of the Balinese, together with the successful export of Balinese musical practice to the rest of the world, make a compelling case for the continued vitality of the tradition.

Appendix

Baris *score in standard Western notation.*

Selected Sonography

Since the 1920s, when recordings of gamelan sparked Colin McPhee into going to Bali, there has been a steady stream of international releases. Older ones varied in quality and accuracy of representation. Many recent issues feature improved recording quality, are careful to include complete compositions and ensembles, and provide well-researched notes. A selection of the best ones currently available follows:

Auvidis Ethnic label:
B 6769 *Bali: Musiques du Nord-Ouest*

Auvidis Unesco label:
D 8059 *Bali: Court Music and Banjar Music*
D 8003 *Bali: Folk Music*

Buda Records label:
92601-2 *Anthologie des musiques de Bali, Traditions Populaires*
92602-2 *Anthologie des musiques de Bali, Gamelans Virtuoses*
92603-2 *Anthologie des musiques de Bali, Musiques Rituelles*
92604-2 *Anthologie des musiques de Bali, Traditions Savantes*

CMP label:
CD 3003 *Gamelan Batel Wayang Ramayana*
CD 3008 *Gamelan Semar Pegulingan Saih Pitu*
CD 3011 *Jegog: The Bamboo Gamelan of Bali*

King label (fine recordings, albeit poorly annotated):
KICC 5126 *Gamelan Music of Bali*
KICC 5127 *Music of Bali*
KICC 5128 *Kecak and Sanghyang of Bali*
KICC 5154 *Gamelan Gong Kebyar "Eka Cita"*
KICC 5157 *Jegog of Negara*
KICC 5156 *Gender Wayang of Sukawati Village*
KICC 5155 *Gamelan Semar Pegulingan of Binoh Village*
KICC 5153 *Gamelan Gong Gde of Batur Temple*
KICC 5182 *Gamelan Selonding "Guna Winangun"*
KICC 5180 *Gamelan Semar Pegulingan "Gunung Jati"*
KICC 5181 *Gamelan Joged Bumbung "Suar Agung"*
KICC 5183 *Geguntangan Arja "Arja Bon Bali"*
KICC 5195 *"Golden Rain" Gong Kebyar Gunung Sari*
KICC 5196 *Saron of Singapadu, Bali*
KICC 5197 *Baleganjur of Pande and Angklung of Sidan*

Long-Distance label:
122119 *Clash of the Gongs (Gamelan Gong Kebyar)*

Lyrichord label:
7406 *Gamelan Semar Pegulingan from the Village of Ketewel*

Nonesuch label:
9 79204-2 *Bali: Gamelan and Kecak*
9 79196-2 *Music from the Morning of the World*
Ocora label:
C560057/58 *Bali: Les Grands Gong Kebyar des Années Soixante*
Rykodisc label:
RCD10315 *Music for the Gods* (historical recordings)
Gamelan Sekar Jaya label:
GSJ-011 *Gamelan Sekar Jaya: Balinese Music in America*
Vital Records:
401 *Music of the Gamelan Gong Kebyar*
402 *Music of the Gamelan Gong Kebyar: works of Nyoman Windha*
[GSJ-011 and Vital 401-2 are available for U.S.$15 plus postage from Wayne Vitale c/o Sekar Jaya, 6485 Conlon Ave., El Cerrito CA, 94530, U.S.A.]
New World Records:
CD 80430-2 *American Works for Balinese Gamelan*
Musicaphon label LPs:
BM30 SL2565 *Panji in Bali I(Gamelan Semar Pegulingan)*
BM30 SL2570 *Ritual Music from Bali I*
BM30 SL2571 *Ritual Music from Bali II*
BM30 SL2573 *Ritual Music from Bali III*
BM30 SL2574 *Ritual Music from Bali IV*
BM30 SL2575 *Contemporary Music from Bali*

Purchasing Cassettes in Bali

Bali Stereo, Aneka and Rick's/Maharani—the three main cassette recording companies in Bali—have, between them, issued many hundreds of tapes documenting just about every kind of music on the island, with the exception of some sacred forms (which, in any case, would be unlikely to generate much interest among the cassette-buying public). The companies' catalogues are constantly growing and business is brisk, especially at shops in urban areas. Master recordings are usually good, but unfortunately the duplication processes and the quality of tape used often results in rather poor and distorted cassettes by the time they arrive at retail stores. Be sure to listen to any tape you wish to buy in the store before you pay for it.

Many of the villages and gamelan genres mentioned in this book are represented by a number of releases. Gamelans from KOKAR and STSI, the music and dance academies, are constantly recorded performing both new music and their renditions of the standard repertoire. The list below, grouped by genre, is highly selective and in fact gets more out of date daily. (NB—Bali Stereo is abbreviated as BS; Aneka as AN, and Rick's/Maharani as MA. Most Maharani cassettes do not have catalogue numbers.)

Gamelan gong kebyar:
Lelambatan Kuno (Gladag village) [BS 639]
Festival Gong Kebyar Se-Bali 1982, Juara I [BS 588]
 (First-prize winners from Angantaka village)

Kreasi Gong Kebyar [AN 551 ASTI (STSI) Vol. 4]
Kreasi Baru Abdi Budaya (Perean village) [AN 242]
Festival Gong Kebyar 1993: Ombak Ing Segara [AN 884]
Festival Gong Kebyar 1995: Sunari [AN 956]
Khusus Karya I Nym. Windha SSKar: Kreasi Pilihan [BS 834]

Gamelan semar pegulingan/pelegongan:
Tabuh Klasik Semar Pegulingan (Binoh village) [BS 350]
Tabuh Bebarongan (Sanur Kauh village) [BS 683]
"Sekar Gadung" Semar Pegulingan Saih Pitu [AN 762 ASTI (STSI) Vol. 15]

Gamelan gender wayang:
Gamelan Gender (Banjar Kayu Mas Kelod, Denpasar) [BS 643-644]
The Best of Gamelan Gender (Sukawati village) [MA 20]

Gamelan angklung:
Angklung Sidan (Sidan village) [BS 294]
Angklung Kocok [AN 606 ASTI (STSI) Vol. 10]
Kreasi Angklung Muda Cinta Sutaji [MA]

Gamelan gong gde:
Gong Agung Sekar Sandat (Sulahaan village) [BS 421]

Gamelan joged bumbung/tingklik:
Kreasi Joged (Samblong village) [AN 617]
Nice + Easy Rindik [MA 23]

Gamelan jegog:
Tabuh Jegog "Makepung" (Sangkaragung village) [AN 611]
Kreasi Tabuh Seni Jegog, Putera Ardana Kusuma (Bilupoh village) [MA]

Gamelan gambang:
Gambang Pitra Yadnya (Banjar Bedhe, Tabanan) [AN 410]

Gamelan selonding:
Selonding Kreasi Baru (STSI Academy) [BS 755]
Best of Gamelan Selonding, Vols. 1 & 2 (Tenganan village) [MA]

Gamelan luang:
Kreasi Gong Luwang (Kerambitan Village) [BS 749]

Gamelan bebonangan/beleganjur:
Kreasi Beleganjur (Banjar Kaliungu Kaja, Denpasar) [BS 720]
Juara I Lomba Beleganjur Badung 1987; Sekaa Gong Suta Darma (Ubung Kaja village) [MA]

Cak:
Kecak Live [MA]

Other cassettes of interest:
Kekawin Suta Soma (the singing of scriptures) [AN 21]
Gusti Putu Oka: Suling Tunggal (solo flute) [MA]
I Wayan Sinti, M.A.: Solo Rebab [MA]
Kindama: Kreasi Baru Ujian Tingkat Seniman 1985 ASTI. (An excellent modern piece composed for a new type of seven-tone ensemble) [BS 640]

Glossary

angklung (ahng-*kloong*); a bamboo rattle, now uncommon in Bali, that produces a single pitch when shaken.

angsel (ahng-*sul*); a sharp, sudden dance movement or musical accent.

angsel bawak (ahng-*sul* bah-*wahk*); a short angsel that is prepared, executed and completed within two gong cycles.

angsel lantang (ahng-*sul* lahn-*tahng*); a long angsel, prepared, executed and completed over several cycles; usually it is the climax of the performance.

arja (ahr-*jha*); a Balinese theatrical form combining dance, singing, indigenous stories, and comedy.

ASTI See STSI

balai banjar (bah *lay* bahn-*jahr*); the village ward meeting hall, ordinarily the storage and rehearsal space for the gamelan.

Bali Arts Festival A yearly event, held at the Denpasar Art Center in June and July, that was initiated by Balinese Governor Ida Bagus Mantra in 1979 as a showcase for new and traditional performing, literary, culinary and plastic arts.

banjar (bahn-*jahr*); village ward; community organization.

bapang (bah-*pahng*); a colotomic cycle of 4 or 8 beats punctuated in the middle by the kemong.

Baris (bah-*riss*); a genre of male warrior dances; also specifically refers to the solo Baris dance popular today.

Baris cina (bah-*riss* chee-*nha*); a sacred Baris performed only at certain ceremonies in Renon village.

Baris gde (bah-*riss* g'*day*); one of several group Baris choreographies with sacred functions.

Barong (bah-*rong*); the Balinese protector-dragon.

batel (bah-*tell*); battle music; also one of several possible colotomic structures used to underpin such music.

bebende (b'-ben-*day*); a medium sized gong with a flattened boss sometimes used for colotomic punctuation.

byong (bee-*yong*); an explosive kebyar attack which includes the sound of eight reyong pots played together.

cak (cha'); a performance genre portraying a climactic episode from the *Ramayana* epic. A chorus of men surrounding dancers imitate the sounds of a monkey army with percussive noises and interlocking vocal rhythms.

cakepung (cha-k'-*poong*); a choral imitation of the sounds of the gamelan, performed informally in northern and eastern Bali.

Calonarang (cha-lohn-ah-*rhang*); a Balinese tale of sorcery and possession performed as a drama, usually with gamelan pelegongan accompaniment.

calung (cha-*loong*); the middle-register instrument that plays the core melody tones.

cengceng (cheng-*cheng*); a set of small cymbals used in most gamelans.

cengceng kopyak (cheng-*cheng* ko-*pya'*); large crash cymbals used in ceremonial music.

colotomy; colotomic structure the technique of using gongs to mark important structural points in music; the arrangement of gong strokes in a given melody.

condong (chohn-*dong*); attendant to a princess or queen, a character found in many performance genres, notably the legong keraton dances.

dag (dhag); the deep sound made with either a panggul (mallet) or the palm of the right hand on the kendang wadon.

dalang (dah-*lhang*); storyteller or puppeteer.

ding, dong, deng dung, dang solfege names of the tones in Balinese tuning systems.

dolanan (do-*lahn*-an); children's songs and song-games.

drama gong a theatrical form portraying contemporary stories, popular since the 1960s.

dug (doog); the deep sound (but not so deep as dag) made with a panggul (mallet) playing on the right head of the kendang lanang.

Festival Gong the yearly Bali-wide gamelan gong kebyar competition.

gabor (gah-*bohr*); a genre of female offering dances. Also called Pendet in some areas.

gamelan (gah-*mel*-an); set of instruments; orchestra.

gamelan angklung a delicate four-tone ensemble used mainly in temple ceremonies and processions.

gamelan bebonangan (b'-bo-*nang*-an); a marching gamelan with gongs, drums and cymbals.

gamelan beleganjur (b'-le-*ghan*-joor); see gamelan bebonangan.

gamelan gambang (gam-*bahng*); an ancient and sacred seven-tone ensemble using four wooden-keyed instruments and two metal sarons. (See also saron.)

gamelan gambuh (gam-*booh*); one of the oldest extant gamelan types. The ensemble is comprised of large flutes, rebab, and percussion; it accompanies theatrical settings of old Javanese stories.

gamelan gandrung (gan-*droong*); a once-popular bamboo ensemble used to accompany street dances.

gamelan gender wayang (g'n-*dare* wah-*yang*); four-piece, slendro-tuned ensemble used mainly to accompany the shadow play.

gamelan gong bheri (bh'*ree*); a gamelan of gongs and drums found only in the village of Renon and used to accompany the Baris cina dance.

gamelan gong a scaled-down version of the gamelan gong gde that was common during the decades prior to the emergence of kebyar.

gamelan gong gde (g'-*day*); the largest Balinese gamelan, important in the courts during the feudal era.

gamelan gong kebyar (k'-*byahr*); the standard modern concert gamelan, important for both sacred and secular functions.

gamelan jegog (j'-*gog*); a 4-tone gamelan made from gigantic stalks of bamboo, found solely in the western district of Jembrana.

gamelan joged bumbung (jo-*ged* boom-*boong*); a slendro-tuned bamboo ensemble that plays instrumental music and accompanies the joged dance.

gamelan luang (lwang); a rare and sacred seven-tone ensemble.

gamelan pelegongan (p' le-*gong*-an); a five-tone derivative of the gamelan Semar Pegulingan used mainly in accompanying the legong kraton dances.

gamelan selonding (s' lohn-*ding*); a sacred gamelan of iron keys, found in many eastern Bali Aga villages.

gamelan Semar Pegulingan (s'*mar* p'-goo-*ling*-ahn); a bronze seven-tone ensemble of the royal courts; also a five-tone version of the same.

gangsa (gahng-sah); a middle-register metallophone used to play melodic ornamentation.

gegaboran (g' gah-*bohr*-an); a colotomic structure used in Gabor dance forms and tari lepas (see Gabor).

gender (g'n-*dare*); any metallophone constructed so that the keys are suspended over bamboo resonators; more specifically the term is used to connote genders that are played with two mallets, one in each hand.

gending (g'n-*ding*); musical composition.

genggong (g'n-*gong*); a kind of jew's harp.

gilak (ghee-*lahk*); a colotomic pattern important in male dances and processional music.

gineman (ghee-*num*-an); a rhapsodic, free introduction to an instrumental composition.

gotong royong (go-tong row-*yohng*); mutual help, community service.

grantang (gran-*tahng*); see tingklik.

jauk (jowk); a masked dance portraying a demonic character.

jegogan (j' *go*-gahn); the deepest-toned keyed instruments; used to stress important notes in the core melody.

jublag (joo-*blag*); alternate name for the calung.

kabupaten (kha-boo-pah-*ten*); government region or district. Bali has eight; they are Badung, Bangli, Buleleng, Gianyar, Jembrana, Karangasem, Klungkung, and Tabanan.

kajar (kha-*jahr*); (from the verb ajar, to teach) a colotomic instrument that mimics drum rhythms in some styles of music.

kantilan (kahn-*teel*-an); the highest-pitched instruments in the gangsa section.

kap the slapping sound made with the left hand on the kendang wadon.

kebyar (k'-*byahr*); abbreviation for gamelan gong kebyar or its music; also a violent, rhythmically irregular passage played by a full gamelan in unison.

Kebyar Duduk (dhoo-*dhook*); A tari lepas choreographed by Maria in the 1920s that is performed in a sitting position.

Kebyar Trompong (trohm-*pong*); A tari lepas choreographed by Maria in which the dancer performs on the trompong.

kecak (khe-cha'); see cak.

kekawin (k' kah-*win*); vocal music sung from texts in palm-leaf manuscripts and written in Kawi, the old Javanese language.

kelenang (k' le-*nahng*); tiny colotomic instrument that falls between beats in some older styles of music.

kemong (k' *mohng*); small hanging gong often used to mark the midpoints of melodies.

kempli (k' m-*plee*); horizontal gong, hand held or mounted on a stand, that is primarily used to keep a steady beat.

kempur (k' m-*poor*); medium sized hanging gong that is used to demarcate important structural points in melodies.

kendang (k 'n-*dahng*); the cylindrical, two-headed Balinese drum, held across the lap and played with both hands.

kendang mabarung (m' *bah*-roong); an ensemble featuring gigantic drums that is popular in west Bali.

kerawang (k' rah-*wang*); the bronze alloy used in casting gongs and keys.

kerawitan (k' rah-wee-*tahn*); a general term for the art of gamelan and gamelan music.

ketua sekaha gong (k' twa s' kha gong); administrative head of a gamelan club.

kidung (khee-*dhoong*); a type of sacred vocal music based mostly on old Balinese poetry; also the singing style associated with kidung.

KOKAR/SMKI the Balinese high school of the performing arts, located in Batubulan.

kotekan (kho-te'-ahn); melodic ornamentation composed of two interlocking musical parts. (See also polos, sangsih)

kreasi baru (k' ray-ah-si bah-*rhoo*); new compositions or choreographies.

lagu (lah-*ghoo*); melody.

lanang (lah-*nhang*); male. Refers to the higher-pitched of a pair of gongs or drums. eg., kendang lanang, gong lanang. (See also wadon)

Lasem (lah-*s'm*); a Javanese legend enacted in one of the legong choreographies; also the name of a lelambatan composition in tabuh kutus form.

latihan (lah-*tee*-han); a rehearsal. (Indonesian)

legong bidedari (l' *gong* bee-d' *dah*-ree); a progenitor of the legong keraton performed in Ketewel village.

legong keraton (l' *gong* k' rah-*tohn*); a group of classical dance suites performed by pairs of young girls or women, often performed with a prelude danced by the condong.

lelambatan (l' lahm-*bha*-tahn); a family of classical instrumental compositions performed primarily in the temple to entertain visiting deities.

Listibiya (lis-*tih*-b'ya); the Balinese Government Council on the Arts.

lontar (lohn-*tahr*); palm leaf manuscripts.

mabarung (m' *bah*-roong); to play together in competition style.

muruk (moo-*roo'*); a rehearsal. (Balinese)

nangka or **ketewel** (nahng-kha); an indigenous semi-hard wood used to carve drums and instrument frames.

nuutin (n 'woo-*tin*); (from the verb tuut, to follow) a simple kotekan pattern in which the sangsih alternates with the polos on the next highest tone.

odalan (o-*dahl*-ahn); Balinese temple anniversary ceremonies. They occur once in each 210 day calendrical cycle and are marked by three days of festivities that often include music and dance performances.

Oleg Tambulilingan (o-leg tahm-boo-*lil*-ing-ahn); a choreography of Maria's from the early 1950s depicting the courtship of two bumblebees in a garden of flowers.

oncang-oncangan (ohn-*chahng* ohn-*chahng*-ahn); percussive interjections in kebyar music created by the composite sounds of drums, cengceng, and eight of the reyong pots played together to form a chord.

pak (pah'); the slapping sound made with the left hand on the kendang lanang.

panggul (pahng-*gool*); mallet.

pelawah (p' lah-*wah*); wooden musical instrument frame.

pelog (peh *lohg*); a seven tone tuning system, with many five-tone derivatives, that is used throughout Bali and Java.

pemade (p' mah-*day*); the middle-range instruments of the gangsa section.

pemungkah (p' moong-*kah*); opening music for the shadow play, performed while the dalang introduces the puppets to the world of the screen.

penabuh (p' nah-*booh*); gamelan musician (see also tabuh)

pengawak (p' ng-ah-*wa'*); (from awak, body) main movement of a musical composition.

penyacah (p' nyah-*chah*); an instrument used in some gamelans that is one octave higher than the calung and plays at twice their rate.

polos (po-*lohss*); the component of kotekan that is closely related to the core melody tones. (See also sangsih, kotekan)

preret (p' ray-*ret*); a reedy trumpet found in east Bali and Lombok.

Rangda (rhang-*dha*); witch-mother; nemesis of the barong.

rebab (r' *bahb*); a two-string bowed instrument.

rejang (r' *jahng*); a sacred ceremonial dance for women.

reyong (r' *yhong*); instrument consisting of a row of tuned small gongs arranged in scalar order on a long frame that is played by pairs of musicians. The reyong in the gamelan gong kebyar is played by four people.

rindik (rin-*dhi'*); see tingklik.

sangsih (sahng-*sih*); the component of kotekan that is created by interlocking with the polos. (See also kotekan, polos)

saron (sah-*rhon*); any metallophone constructed so that the keys are held in place by posts and laid over a trough. (Also called gangsa jongkok.)

sekaha (s' *kha*); club or organization.

seledet (s' le-*deht*); dance movement consisting of a rapid side-to-side flick of the eyes.

selisir (s' lee-*sihr*); one of the five-tone modes derived from the pelog tuning system.

sendratari (s' n-dra-*tah*-ree); dance-drama; a modern amalgam of traditional stories and a variety of music and dance types.

sisya (see-sya); in the *Calonarang* story, the apprentices of the sorceress.

slanketan (s' lahn-k'-*tahn*); an ornamentation style of the gamelan jegog.

slendro (s' len-*dhro*); a tuning system found throughout Java and Bali that is theoretically based on the division of the octave into five equal parts.

STSI   until recently known as ASTI; the government college/conservatory of the performing arts in Denpasar.

suling (soo-ling); bamboo flute.

sunaren (soo-nah-*rhen*); one of the five-tone modes derived from the Pelog tuning system.

tabuh (ta-*booh*); composition, musical form, also used as a verb (menabuh) meaning 'to play'. (see also penabuh)

taksu (tahk-*soo*); performance charisma. Balinese believe in an individual's innate, inherited ability to make an audience enjoy a performance.

tari lepas (tah-ree l' *pahss*); (lit. free dances) brief modern dances unconnected to larger theatrical forms.

tawa-tawa a small gong used in the gamelan angklung.

tektekan (te'-*te*'-ahn); ensemble similar to gamelan beleganjur using bamboo sticks instead of or in addition to gongs and cengceng.

tembang (t' m-*bahng*); a family of verse forms.

tembung (t' m-buhng); one of the five-tone modes derived from the pelog tuning system.

Teruna Jaya (t' roo-nah jah-*yha*); a tari lepas depicting the capricious moods of a youth on the verge of adulthood.

tingklik (ting-*kli*'); an instrument of bamboo tubes suspended in a wooden frame; also known as grantang or rindik.

topeng (to-*peng*); masked dance.

trompong (trohm-*pong*); instrument consisting of a row of tuned small gongs arranged in scalar order on a long frame that is played by a single musician.

tukang (too-*khang*); someone that performs an activity. Tukang kendang: drummer; tukang reyong; reyong player; etc.

tut (toot); the deep sound (but not so deep as dag) made with the palm of the right hand on the kendang lanang.

ugal (oo-*ghal*); the lead gangsa.

wadon (wah-*dohn*); female. Refers to the lower-pitched of a pair of gongs or drums, eg., kendang wadon, gong wadon. (See also lanang)

wayang kulit (wah-yhang koo-*lit*); the shadow puppet play.

Selected Bibliography

Books—General

Baum, Vicki: *Tale of Bali* (Geoffrey Bles, London, 1937; Reprinted by Oxford-in-Asia, 1973)

Coast, John: *Dancing Out of Bali*—also printed as *Dancers of Bali*—(G.P. Putnam, New York, 1953)

Covarrubias, Miguel: *Island of Bali* (A. Knopf, Inc., New York, 1937; Reprinted by Oxford-In-Asia, 1972)

McPhee, Colin: *A House in Bali* (John Day, New York, 1946; Reprinted by Oxford-In-Asia, 1972)

McPhee, Colin: *A Club of Small Men* (John Day, New York, 1948)

Ramseyer, Urs: *The Art and Culture of Bali* (Oxford Press, Singapore, 1977)

Also note the following two introductions to Javanese music:

Lindsay, Jennifer: *Javanese Gamelan* (Oxford Press, Singapore, 1979)

Sorrell, Neil: *A Guide to the Gamelan* (Faber and Faber, London, 1990)

Books—Technical

Bandem, I Made: *Wayang Wong in Contemporary Bali* (Unpublished Ph.D. Dissertation, Wesleyan University, 1980)

Bandem, I Made, and DeBoer, Frederik: *Kaja and Kelod: Balinese Dance in Transition* (Oxford Press, Kuala Lumpur, 1981)

De Zoete, Beryl, and Spies, Walter: *Dance and Drama in Bali* (Faber and Faber Ltd., London, 1938; Reprinted by Oxford-in-Asia, 1973)

Lansing, J. Stephen: *The Three Worlds of Bali* (Praeger Scientific Studies, New York, 1983)

McPhee, Colin: *Music in Bali: A Study in Form and Instrumental Organization* (Yale University Press, New Haven, 1966)

Oja, Carol: *Colin McPhee (1900-1964): A Composer in Two Worlds* (Smithsonian Press, 1990)

Ornstein, Ruby: *Gamelan Gong Kebyar: The Development of a Balinese Musical Tradition* (Unpublished Ph.D. Dissertation, UCLA, 1971)

Schlager, Ernst: *Rituelle Siebenton-Musik Auf Bali* (A. Francke AG Verlag Bern, 1976)

Wallis, Richard: *The Voice as a Mode of Cultural Expression in Bali* (Unpublished Ph.D. Dissertation, U. Michigan Ann Arbor, 1981)

Articles

Bandem, I Made: "Indonesia" (section on Bali) in *Grove's Dictionary of Music and Musicians*, London, 1983

Belo, Jane, Editor: *Traditional Balinese Culture*; Articles by Bateson, Holt, McPhee, Mead, Mershon and other ethnographers working in Bali in the 1930s. (Columbia University Press, New York, 1970)

Eisman, Fred and Margaret: *Sekala/Niskala*, a collection of writings on Balinese culture—with a few pertaining to music—published privately by the author and also by Periplus Editions, Singapore, 1989.

Hood, Mantle: "The Challenge of Bi-Musicality" (*SEM Journal*, Vol. 4, 1960, pp. 55-59)

Hood, Mantle: "Balinese Semar Pegulingan: The Modal System" (*Progress Reports in Ethnomusicology*, Vol. 3 No. 2, 1990)

Keeler, Ward: "A Musical Journey Through Java and Bali" (*Indonesia Journal*, 1975)

McPhee, Colin: "The Balinese Gender Wayang and its Music" (*Djawa XVI/1*, 1936; Reprinted in Belo, Jane, *Traditional Balinese Culture*—see above)

McPhee, Colin: "Children and Music in Bali" (Djawa XVIII/6, 1936; Reprinted in Belo, Jane, *Traditional Balinese Culture*—see above)

Schaareman, D. "The Gamelan Gambang of Tatulingga, Bali" (*SEM Journal*, September 1980, pp. 465-482)

Seebass, T. "A Note on Kebyar in Modern Bali" (*Orbis Musicae, vol. IX*, 1978, pp. 103-121)

Toth, A. "The Gamelan Luang of Tangkas, Bali" (*UCLA Selected Reports in Ethnomusicology*, 1975 Vol. II No. 2, pp. 65-79)

Finally, the American Gamelan Institute publishes the periodical Balungan, (Jody Diamond, Director and Editor-in-Chief) which caters to the growing number of gamelan enthusiasts worldwide and contains articles relating exclusively to gamelan music in both new and traditional forms. Balungan is a Javanese word that means, roughly, 'core melody'. The Institute also maintains an archive of recordings and publications. For sample copies and further information, contact:

The American Gamelan Institute
Box A-36
Hanover, NH 03755
U.S.A.

Index